BEGINNER'S DICTIONARY

of

CONTEMPORARY

INTERNATIONAL RELATIONS

=

Bhaso Ndzendze

ISBN: 978-0-620-74467-6
Published in 2017 by
The National Library of South Africa (NLSA).
225 Johannes Ramokhoase Street
Pretoria, 0001

For E.N. Ndzendze

CONTENTS

INTRODUCTION

=

Upon completing the first of what may be called a real dictionary in 1755, A *Dictionary of the English Language* (there'd been earlier attempts of course, but none quite as concise as his), Dr Samuel Johnson was granted a rather strange visit by a group of aristocratic women. They had come, they said, to congratulate him on his *Dictionary* and, further, they were especially grateful to him for leaving out all improper and profane words from his publication. Dr Johnson's response was just as amusing: he happily expressed his gratitude that they had taken so much effort in looking for the improper and profane words. This is a telling little account; indeed, there is scarcely anything in the intellectual space which does not have the capacity to be insulting.

The discipline of International Relations is a highly contested one and is therefore no exception to this rule of thumb. Dealing, as it does, with human actions, designs and attitudes – and being tied, as it is, into the great questions of power and legitimacy – the field is necessarily complex and characterised by disagreement as well as "disjuncture" to borrow from one of its finest living practitioners, Arjun Appadurai.

Therefore, it should be made clear that the definitions here are not the only ones, neither could they intend to be. Nevertheless, for better or for worse, words (especially when printed and contained within the pages of something calling itself a dictionary) tend to gain an air of objective truthfulness and charm far from the amount deserved. But the idea of grand-standing truth is perhaps a relic of a time gone by. As a dictionary not of lexicon and grammar but of world politics, this one can entertain such hopes even less. But much effort has been made in this pursuit.

Bhaso Ndzendze, January 17 2017

Mthatha, South Africa

DEFINITIONS

0-9

9/11 attacks.

The first foreign attack on US soil since Pearl Harbour in 1941, the attacks took place in New York City on the 11th of September (9/11) and saw the destruction of the World Trade Center twin towers and the Pentagon in Washington D.C., and massive loss of life with current estimates placing the death-toll at 2,977. Al-Qaeda (see below) leader Osama bin Laden soon claimed responsibility for the attacks, which were carried out when 19 al-Qaeda members hijacked two planes and drove them directly into the buildings. The attacks are seen as a watershed moment in international relations since the end of the Cold War (see below), as they saw then US President George W. Bush engage the country in a polarising and controversial "war on terror" (see below) that saw the invasion of Afghanistan in 2001 and a more controversial one of Iraq in 2003 under the pretext of pre-emptive war (see below) against that country, about which it was claimed (but later unproved) by the Bush administration that it had weapons of mass destruction with which it was going to sponsor al-Qaeda and other terrorist organisations.

9/11 Commission.

Set up in the wake of the 9/11 attacks in the US (see above), it was established to ascertain what made the occurrence of the attacks possible. The Commission's report, concluded in 2004, stated that there was a lack of preparation on the part of the US intelligence and law-enforcement agencies. Also significant was the report's establishment that there was no plausible link between the Saddam Hussein regime in Iraq, and al-Qaeda (see below), the terrorist organisation which claimed responsibility for the attacks – a claim which had been used by the US government to invade Iraq in 2003. See http://9-11commission.gov/

Aa

Abenomics.

Is a term used to refer to the economic policies introduced by Prime Minister Shinzo Abe in order to steer the Japanese economy from the long recessionary path it has been taking. Abenomics has consisted of three particular policies: (1) quantitative easing; (2) lowering of taxes and (3) internal structural adjustments in the Japanese economy. The Japanese economy, which has seen slow and sometimes negative yearly growth since the late 1990s, and has been characterised by increasing unemployment, declining trade levels, has so far been slow to respond to the reforms. While the quarterly earnings were positive and stock markets saw growth in early 2013, the year the reforms were introduced, the reforms also resulted in the devaluation of the Japanese currency, the yen; thereby somewhat impairing Japan's buying power to purchase foreign goods such as natural resources and food. The government has in turn characterised this is a short-term setback that will pay-off at a later stage.

African Peer Review Mechanism (APRM).

Seeking to encourage a proliferation of transparency and democracy generally seen to be lacking on the African continent, in 2003 the African Peer-Review

Mechanism was established as part of the New Partnership for Africa's Development (NEPAD; see below). The mechanism is a voluntary one to which various heads of African states, so far numbering 33, accede to self-rate on a set questionnaire and to be rated by their fellow leaders on how their policies and regimes measure in terms of democracy and political governance, economic governance and management, corporate governance, and socio-economic development. While widely praised as an innovation, the effectiveness of the mechanism has been called into question due to its voluntariness. See also Human Development Index (HDI).

African Development Bank (AfDB).

Formed in 1964, it is a development focused financial institution comprised of 78 African and non-African member states and invests in member countries' projects that seek longer term economic development and poverty alleviation, such as water, transport, sanitation and communications projects. The Bank has invested in some 2,885 projects amounting to a total of over $47-billion. The three largest shareholders in the Bank's board of directors are the European Union, Nigeria, the US and Japan.

African Growth and Opportunity Act (AGOA).

Brought into existence by the Clinton administration, it gave sub-Saharan African countries unprecedented access to the US market. Concessions included preferential tariff-free import by African countries of over 30 goods. In turn, the US gained further access to African markets with various consequences for employment, and inflation as seen in the crowding out of domestic African markets such as the poultry industry. Critics point to this development and, further, the alleged usage of AGOA by the US as a coercive means to dictate to African countries in important international (and sometimes domestic) issues such as in the resolution-forming votes in the UN Security Council (see below). See also Yemen precedent.

African Union.

A 52-member body of African states established in 1963 as the Organisation for African Unity (OAU) and renamed in 2000 as the African Union. Has as its duties the coordination of health, security and economic development policies among African states. It has been criticised of not doing enough to curb human rights abuses, insurgency and violence in the continent, and of being mechanically constrained in responding to poverty. One of its most prominent contemporary plans is the 'Agenda 2063', according to which it intends to increase food security, gender equality, youth employment, and regional integration in Africa. See also Pan-Africanism.

Afrobarometer.

A surveying mechanism managed and published by various institutions in sub-Saharan Africa. Its research aims at finding out sub-Saharan African citizens' attitude(s) towards certain events and concepts, and it thereby articulates better the social and political atmosphere in the subcontinent.

Al-Qaeda.

A terrorist organisation whose name means 'the Base', it was founded in 1988 by the son of billionaire businessman Osama bin Laden, a citizen of Saudi Arabia. It pledges allegiance to the Sunni branch of Islam, and avowedly seeks the creation of a theocratic regime ran according to Islamic doctrine. Ironically funded by the US Central Intelligence Agency (CIA) in its early days as an ally against the Soviet Union in the Middle East, it claimed responsibility for the New York attacks on 9/11 (see above) as well as various other US-targeted attacks, most notably the 1998 US embassy bombings. It has numerous international branches and operates worldwide and has staged or inspired suicide bombings (its main tactic) in such disparate parts of the world as North America, Norway, East Africa and the Middle East. Relations between al-Qaeda and the two other most prominent terrorist organisations, the Taliban and ISIS (see below), are ambiguous but it is generally considered to not be friendly with the latter but has collaborated with the former. One of the principal targets of the US War on Terror, US President Barack Obama stated that the US military killed leader Osama bin Laden on the 11th of May, 2011 in Pakistan where he was in hiding. Its activities have been criticised by many mainstream, moderate Muslims.

Al-Shabaab.

A Somali branch of al-Qaeda (see above) formed in 2006 that gained fame for its responsibility for the 2013 attack in Westgate Mall in Nairobi, Kenya in which 67 people were killed and 175 were injured by gunfire. Upon being pushed back by a US-backed Somalian militia, it retreated to the countryside and controls some rural parts of the country.

American Sniper.

Produced by Clint Eastwood and starring Bradley Cooper, it is a controversial 2014 film depicting the life and career of an American military veteran of the Iraqi War. It was particularly controversial because, while Eastwood is an ardent critic of the US invasion of Iraq in 2003, the film legitimised the war by portraying the main character in war in the deserts of Iraq immediately after seeing news of the 9/11 attacks on television. Doing so created a false timeline in which the US invaded Iraq because of a supposed connection with the 9/11 attacks, something which has never been proven. The film therefore served to justify a controversial pre-emptive war and "liberation" of Iraq whose taking place is hotly debated.

Amnesty International.

International, non-government information-gathering and human rights advocacy group, it compiles annual reports on the state of political freedom in countries all over the world. See http://www.amnesty.org/

Anarchy.

Refers to the lack of a world government outside of the voluntary principles and organisations which states abide by. A natural outcome of this is the constellated pursuit of individual national interests by the various state and non-state actors which may or may not lead to conflict or co-operation. See also global governance, realism.

Annan, Kofi.

Ghanaian diplomat who served as the United Nations General Secretary between 1997 and 2006, and founder of the Kofi Annan Foundation. His achievements as General Secretary of the UN include combating the HIV/AIDS epidemic, and setting the Millennium Development Goals agenda (see below). Controversy brewed after the Oil-for-Food programme became mired in scandal, but his name was cleared. Received the Nobel Peace Prize in 2001 on his own behalf as well as that of the UN when they were both awarded for work in battling the HIV/AIDS epidemic, terrorism and enhancing human rights and development.

Annexation.

A scenario whereby one state takes over the territory of another state. The most recent such incidence was the Russian annexation of Crimea in 2014 (see below).

Antarctic Treaty System.

Refers to the conditions agreed upon by states signing the 1959 Antarctic Treaty. These include the banning of military activity, nuclear waste disposal and mining in the continent of Antarctica and the promotion of scientific and conservatory research and efforts. Currently, 50 states are party to the treaty.

Appeasement.

Refers to the granting of gains to an aggressor state in the hopes that doing so will avert actual conflict. Appeasement was most famously, and controversially, applied in 1938 when Adolf Hitler was allowed by Britain, then under the leadership of Prime Minister Neville Chamberlain, to annex (see above) Czechoslovakia. Allowing Nazi Germany to do so, Chamberlain argued, would guarantee peace in Europe and would help avert another great war on the scale of the one seen between 1914 and 1919. Appeasement came to an end in mid-late 1939 when Nazi Germany invaded Poland and Britain and France finally declared war on the aggressor.

Arab League.

Founded in 1945, currently comprised of 22 Arabic member states. Its self-declared foundational goal is to "draw closer the relations between member States and co-ordinate collaboration between them, to safeguard their independence and sovereignty, and to consider in a general way the affairs and interests of the Arab countries." Its principal arms are the Arab League Educational, Cultural and Scientific Organization (ALESCO) and the Economic and Social Council of the Arab League's Council of Arab Economic Unity (CAEU) through which it pursues interests of the "Arab world" in political, economic and cultural fronts.

Arab Spring.

Beginning with a Tunisian vendor setting himself on fire in protest of the Tunisian regime's abuses in 2010, it quickly became a democracy-seeking movement in the historically non-democratic countries of the Middle East; large protests, many of whom were organised through social media outlets such as Facebook and Twitter, seeking regime change soon broke out in Libya (where Muammar Gaddafi was removed), Yemen (where Ali Abdullah was removed); Morocco, Jordan, Kuwait, Lebanon and Oman (all 5 countries saw major reforms), and minor ones in Bahrain, Saudi Arabia, and Mauritania which were not quite as successful. The uprisings saw different results, ranging from democratisation (e.g., Tunisia and Egypt), civil war (e.g., Libya, Syria, and Yemen, see below) and little to no effect (e.g., Saudi Arabia and Sudan). Nevertheless, the importance of the protests was felt internationally due to the significance of the region as a US strategic interest, a neighbour to both Europe and Africa and an international provider of natural resources, the most important of which is perhaps oil.

Arms dumping.

The process of selling military weapons below market price. A commonly cited example is the selling of such weapons by the US and the former Soviet Union to governments and rebel forces in Africa following the end of the Cold War (see below).

Arnold A. Saltzman Institute of War and Peace Studies.

Based in Columbia University, where it was established by the university's President and future President of the United States Dwight D. Eisenhower, it is one of the most prominent think tanks in the world. Its focus is on the overall dimensions and consequences of war. Organises yearly summits and regularly publishes reports on international affairs. Previous alumni include the founder of modern realism Kenneth Waltz (see below).

Article 9 of the Japanese Constitution.

Following defeat, large-scale human loss, nuclear devastation and national humiliation in World War II (see below), which had been in many ways started by Japan in the pacific region, the nation of Japan enacted a new constitution in 1947 whose 9th article prohibits the state from entering war and barres the state from maintaining an army capable of entering war. Nevertheless, beginning in 2014, the Japanese Self-Defense Force, as that country's military is called, was allowed by the Prime Minister and later parliament to arm itself so as to be able to defend allies as well; in effect, ending a 65-year-old policy of minimum militarisation.

Artificial islands.

Man-made islands constructed for strategic and security purposes. The most ardent constructor of these for military purposes is the People's Republic of China which has built two large enough to operate as military barracks, watchtowers, and aircraft runways.

Asian Development Bank (ADB).

Established in 1966 by 31 Asian states, the Asian Development Bank is the largest regional development bank in Asia and the pacific with 67 members coming from the region and outside. Modelled along similar lines as the World Bank Group (see below), the Bank's largest proportional stakeholders are Japan, the United States, China, India and Australia who between themselves own up to 50% of the weighed vote. The ADB's main goals are assisting states in the region with infrastructural development, healthcare, financial systems and sustainable development in the face of climate change. The ADB played a somewhat pivotal role in the emergence of Asian economies in the latter half of the twentieth century, and assisted in the mitigation of the 1997 Asian financial crisis when the currencies of the East Asian states declined exponentially.

Association of Southeast Asian Nations (ASEAN).

A 10-member regional organisation founded in 1967; composed of Brunei, Cambodia, Indonesia, Laos, Malaysia, Myanmar, the Philippines, Thailand, Singapore and Vietnam. Its principal goal is enhancing economic progress for its member states, and maintaining peace in the region. Has been criticised of impunity in human rights abuses in one of its members, Myanmar.

Asteroid mining.

A projected form of mining which will involve extracting mineral resources from asteroids in outer space. So far it has not proved feasible but governments and private enterprises are looking into realising it. See also Mars colonisation project.

Atlanticism.

A European foreign policy outlook which emphasises closeness with the US and Canada, and in turn the North Atlantic Treaty Organization (see below). In the British context it means an embracing and accentuation of the historic and so-called "special" Anglo-American relationship shared by the United Kingdom and the US. British and other Eurosceptics (see below) have highlighted looking to the US as a viable and more attractive alternative to the European Union which they deem inefficient and unconducive to the trade and security which alliance with the US ostensibly brings.

Austrian neutrality.

Since 1955, when the Allies ended their occupation of Austria, the constitution of that country commits it to "everlasting neutrality," though it later joined the European Union which has some continent-wide military measures, such as the Common Security and Defense Policy (CSDP; see below) which require participation by every member.

Autarky.

Refers to a trade and foreign policy which is characterised by the pursuit of eliminating imports from other states. Reasons for autarky vary; they may arise from political reasons such as embargoes (see below), economic reasons induced by a desire to bolster domestic infant industries. North Korea (see below) is an example of a state known for its pursuit of autarky, though it has continued to have some minor but significant trade relations with China and the European Union (see below). See also import substitution and industrialisation (ISI), isolationism, trade deficit, trade surplus.

'Axis of Evil'. A controversial and highly criticised term used by the George W. Bush administration to refer to states it deemed a danger to US national security due to their alleged nuclear weaponry acquisition as well as supposed links with anti-US terrorist organisations. These states were Iran, Iraq, and North Korea (see below).

Bb

Balance of power theory.

Refers to the long-standing realist assumption that in so far as there is no single state powerful enough to dominate others, war may be averted. The theory argues that if a state is powerful enough, it will consequently be tempted by its position and become a war-monger. A cardinal pillar of diplomacy since most explicitly the seventeenth and eighteenth centuries, it informed a series of coalitions against Napoleon I of France (see below) from 1799 to 1815, and some argue that it informs the impetus for the European Union (see below).

Ban Ki-moon.

South Korean politician and diplomat who served as the United Nations General Secretary between 2007 and 2016. While in office, his most notable pursuits were his pushing for more action to curb climate change, and for gaining entry for 26,000 UN peacekeeping forces into civil war-torn Sudan following the Darfur massacre (see below).

Bandung Conference, 1955.

The first international conference to see African and Asian politicians seating together (in Bandung, Indonesia), it was attended by states who chose to not be aligned either with the United States and the

West nor with the Soviet Union during the Cold War (see below). Its themes were the need for rapid decolonisation, sovereignty and independence for African and Asian states that were still under colonialism at the time of the conference.

Beijing Consensus.

This is the name given to a particular form of international engagement and "doing business" by the People's Republic of China. While broad, this concept refers primarily to China's willingness to not stipulate reforms in the domestic structures of the countries it invests in, unlike the International Monetary Fund (see below) and World Bank (see below). Proponents normally compare it to the Washington Consensus which is deemed less tolerant and whose investments are normally accompanied by conditions concerning the domestic policies and practices of the state in which it is investing.

Benelux Union.

Established in 1944, it is a trading and judiciary union between the three neighbouring constitutional monarchy states of Belgium, the Netherlands, and Luxembourg who historically have been under the same government at some point or another. Apart from trade, the union's duties revolve around legislation, especially regarding intellectual property law. The ascendency of the European Union (see below), in which all three Benelux states are members, has limited the scope of the Benelux Union. Headquarters based in Brussels.

Bilateral investment treaty (BIT).

An agreement between two governments for mutual or one-way investment of one country in another. Terms of investing differ but can be controversial; such as the provision of terms in a 1959 bilateral investment of West Germany to Pakistan which allowed German companies in Pakistan to abide by German laws rather than Pakistani laws.

Bipolar international order.

An international state of affairs in which there are two discernible superpower nations that dominate the rest and whose (sometimes conflicting) interests may come to shape global politics. The Cold War (see below) was such an international order. Also see unipolar international order.

Bismarck, Otto von.

German diplomat born in 1815, the year the Napoleonic Wars (see below) were put to a final end, he dominated Prussian and European affairs as the Prussian and later German Chancellor. Unifying the smaller states into the German Empire under Prussian domination and to Austrian exclusion, he forged an alliance system which, from the 1870s onwards, ensured that large-scale war would not take place for a very long time and Europe – at peace within itself – was able to look outward once more and colonised the rest of the world; the colonial conference was hosted by Bismarck in Berlin in 1889. An instinctive conservative statesman loyal to his monarch, king and then Emperor Friedrich Wilhelm, he is remembered for his results-based system of *realpolitik*, a direct outshoot of realism (see below) in foreign policy.

Boko Haram.

Insurgency group that claims alignment to Islam, and avowedly bent on forging a theocratic regime fashioned on the Noble Quran in Nigeria. It came into international attention when its members abducted over 200 young school girls with the intention of selling them off, thus launching the #BringBackOurGirls campaign which called on rapid action for the return of the schoolchildren. For some, the abduction also highlighted a lack of coordination in the Nigerian and west African security forces, as well a lacklustre response by the international community in terms of assisting in the search for the students and elimination of Boko Haram.

Bono.

Real name Paul David Hewson. Irish musician and well known global philanthropist. He has raised funds for causes in sub-Saharan Africa, and has brought the plight of many impoverished and AIDS-afflicted African communities into world attention. Critics question the effectiveness of his techniques and question the purity of his motives. His most notable projects include the ONE Campaign and Product Red.

Border dispute.

Territorial contestation between neighbours states over where one country's realm should begin and another's end. Current ongoing disputes include those between government-controlled southern Republic of Cyprus and the Turkish Republic of Northern Cyprus with a UN-controlled buffer zone in-between the two territories to avert violence; China, India and Pakistan over Kashmir; China and India over the Line of Actual Control.

Boycott, Divest, Sanction (BDS).

Established in 2005 by the Palestinian BDS National Committee, it is a controversial global campaign intended on increasing economic and political pressure on Israel through boycotting, divesting from, and sanctioning Israel goods to pressure the state to reverse its occupation of Palestinian territory as well as grant full citizens' rights and Palestinian right of return which is claimed to not be existent. Critics claim that it is an anti-Semitic movement.

Brain drain.

Refers to the large-scale emigration of skilled and educated individuals from their countries of origin. In contemporary times it has especially become a visible pattern with regards to sub-Saharan Africa which has seen a mass exodus of skilled professionals; United Nations (see below) estimates suggest that some 75% of professionals in Ethiopia alone migrated between 1980 and 1991. Particularly prone to emigration have been healthcare professionals. The debate around the relative benefits and losses of brain drain is ongoing. Some highlight as positives the remittances (see below) which are sent back by the expatriates and which sometimes form the backbones of the underdeveloped nations, as well as the technology transfer which is argued to take place when expatriates return home. On the other hand, others highlight the extent to which the emigrants leave a major skills shortage, and the political vacuum created by their absence instead of remaining and fast-tracking political change at home.

Bretton Woods Conference, 1944.

Arranged in order to rebuild Europe after it was utterly destroyed by World War II (see below), it saw the establishment of the International Monetary Fund (see below), and the International Bank for Reconstruction and Development (see below) one of the core bodies of the World Bank (see below), was also established in the conference.

Brexit.

In June of 2016, the United Kingdom held a referendum in which the public was asked whether their country should stay in the European Union (see below) or exit. By a small majority, the people voted to exit, driving the incumbent Prime Minister David Cameron to resign on principle (he had campaigned for continued European Union membership). Arguments for leaving the EU included the fact that British fishers no longer had an exclusive say over their fishing waters, the UK made a membership payment which essentially amounted to £300-million per week to the body which could have been useful elsewhere and essentially they found the EU restrictive as it did not allow for Britain to have new trade agreements with other countries except through the EU itself. A seemingly easy task at first, exiting the European Union would prove immensely difficult for the British government under the leadership of Theresa May who replaced David Cameron as British Prime Minister.

BRICS.

The international economic association of the fastest developing and industrialising states. Composed of Brazil, Russia, India, China and South Africa from whose first letters the name is derived. Between them, the BRICS countries have a population of 3.6-billion people, a combined nominal GDP (see below) of over $16-trillion; they are anticipated to grow by over 5% in 2017. The recent slowdown of the economic growth of these countries as well as the extent to which China accounts for most of the high aggregate figures has been the subject of commentary, as is the inclusion of South Africa whose economic growth (averaging at less than 5% per year since 2009) is surpassed by many other states. The association is in the process of creating a developmental bank which many see as representing a counterhegemonic tide against the World Bank (see below) and the International Monetary Fund (see below).

Brookings Institute.

Established in 1916, the Brookings Institute is an internationally-acclaimed US economic and political research think tank with a focus on international relations. Winner of the University of Pennsylvania 'Think Tank of the Year' every year since 2006 to 2015. Often described as liberal (see below), especially when compared to other think tanks such as the Heritage Foundation and the Hoover Institution (see below). It is the most cited think tank by US media and politicians.

Bush Doctrine.

Refers to the use of pre-emptive war (see below) as a foreign policy (see below) strategy, particularly as practiced by US President George W. Bush's cabinet with regards to terrorism; the invasion of Afghanistan in 2001, and of Iraq in 2003. See also Powell Doctrine, war on terrorism.

"Butter mountains, wine lakes."

This refers to the outcome of a 2009 decision by the European Union (see below) to purchase, among others, 30, 000 tons of butter, sugar, grain and millions of litres of unwanted wine from farmers in order to prevent them suffering a loss due to a decline in prices for dairy products that took place between 2007 and 2008 by nearly 7%. The heaps of stored and eventually dumped butter and wine spillages are where the phrase derives from. It is usually cited as an example of EU inefficiency and protectionism (see below) by Eurosceptics and African farming groups who see themselves as being denied access to the EU market through tariffs and quotas (see below) for the benefit of the protected EU farmers.

Cc

Cabinda.

Officially a province of Angola separated from its home country by a strip of Congolese land, the enclave of Cabinda is an oil-rich territory. Formerly a Portuguese colony, since 1975 Cabinda has been a theatre of a civil war between the Angolan government and secessionist (see below) elements as led by the Front for the Liberation of the Enclave of Cabinda (FLEC) who want it to become an independent state. FLEC maintains a government-in-exile (see below) in Paris, France.

Caliphate.

A majority Muslim state headed by an individual recognised also to be the religious leader of its constituent population called a Caliph. A concept whose historical precedents include the first four leaders of the nascent Muslim community in the Arabian Peninsula and later conquered territories in the decades following 632CE, subsequent figures have claimed to be Caliphs of the Muslim community; present-day example being the self-declared Islamic State in Syria and Iraq (see below). Disagreement over the designation of the next Caliph gave rise to the Shia-Sunni divide (see below).

Camp David Accords.

A set of agreements reached in the Camp David US Presidential resort between then Egyptian President Anwar Sadat and Israeli Prime Minister Menachem Begin in 1978. Achieved with US mediation by President Jimmy Carter, the treaty led to mutual recognition and peace between Egypt and Israel following the 1967 War and the two leaders received the Nobel Peace Prize (see below) for the achievement. Nevertheless, the portion of the treaty which directly concerned the Palestine question (see below) was carved out without consent from Palestinians and was promptly condemned by the United Nations (see below). Egyptian people also shunned the treaty, deeming it an agreement between President Sadat and the State of Israel, and not them and the Israeli people. It nonetheless led to a subsequent relative normalisation of relations between the two parties.

Carbon footprint.

A complex term referring to the amount of carbon dioxide and methane produced by one or more individuals in a given time period. It is a nominal indicator of how much carbon dioxide, a greenhouse gas, has been emitted into the atmosphere. An important figure in the study and combatting of man-made climate change (see below).

Caribbean Community (CARICOM).

A regional organisation with 15 members from the Caribbean region, the Caribbean Community was formed in 1973 with the foundational mandate of fostering economic cooperation, foreign and domestic policy integration among its members. A 2001 treaty established the CARICOM Single Market and Economy with provisions for the elimination of trade restrictions such as tariffs (see below) and quotas (see below). The Caribbean Community also has a European Court of Justice-regulated trade agreement with the European Union (see below) which allows for a mutual and legally reciprocal trade relationship.

Catalan independence movement.

Refers to the ongoing movement for the region of Catalonia, situated on the northwest of Spain which also includes the city of Barcelona, to become an independent and sovereign state. Catalonia, having its own distinct culture and language declared itself independent in 1931 and took advantage of a power vacuum left by the subsequent Spanish civil war (1936-39), but later re-joined it following a deal that would allow autonomy within Spain. The deal was abolished once the government fell onto the hands of a fascist military regime in 1938. Following the death of Spanish dictator Francisco Franco in 1975, the movement gradually gained resurgence to the effect that by 2015 a non-binding referendum, deemed illegal by the Spanish central government, on independence was held in which more than 80% of those asked voted for sovereignty. A widely popular movement that drew over a million pro-independence demonstrators in 2010, those who support it argue that apart from the linguistic and cultural differences, Catalonia should be dependent on economic grounds, for it is the largest economy in the Kingdom of Spain, having averted the Great Recession (see below) which affected much of Spain, and currently having a gross domestic product (see below) the size of Spanish neighbour Portugal. Along with the government of Spain, various leaders of the European Union (see below), of which Spain is a member, and then US President Barack Obama strongly vocalised support for a united Spain with Catalonia in it. Various leaders of the movement have been arrested in connection with extra-legal activities during pro-independence protests, including one in which there was a public burning of a banner bearing the image of the King of Spain, an act which is illegal in that country. Nevertheless, when pro-independence parties held the majority of the seats in the Catalan parliament in 2015, a binding referendum was scheduled to be held in late 2017. It is perhaps the most visible secessionist (see below) movement in contemporary Europe. See also Walloon Movement.

Central Asia.

Refers to a region in the heartland of the Asian continent composed of Kazakhstan, Kyrgyzstan, Tajikistan, Turkmenistan, and Uzbekistan. All of the states were formerly under Russian and later Soviet Union control.

Central Europe.

A geographical reference to the states placed in-between nominal western and eastern Europe. While very much engaged with their western and eastern neighbours, the peoples of this region have also shared a unique history as the bridge between, and occasional centre of, the two ends of the continent in terms of political arrangements, trade, the arts, and military conflict. Due to geographical ambiguity, which countries form central Europe is the subject of debate, however states in this area are generally understood to include Austria, Croatia, Czech

Republic, Germany, Hungary, Liechtenstein, Poland, Slovakia, and Slovenia.

Central Intelligence Agency (CIA).

Established in 1947 under President Harry Truman, it is the US's main intelligence agency. Its activities include international information-gathering related to US national security. A controversial body, its critics deplore its alleged civilian surveillance activities and the agency has been implicated in multiple international incidents such as the removal of socialist democratically-elected Chilean President Salvador Allende and installing General Augusto Pinochet in his place because he would be a US ally in the Cold War (see below). Its role in the disappearance and killing of Congolese Prime Minister Patrice Lumumba in 1961 has been suggested, and a retired former agent confessed to having helped locate and arrest Nelson Mandela in 1962.

Cesaire, Aime.

Born in French-colonised Martinique, he was a staunch and original critic of colonialism. His most famous work is his *Discourse on Colonialism* published in 1950. Apart from Frantz Fanon (see below), he was perhaps the most influential anticolonial intellectual of the 20th century. His works are still studied in most Postcolonialism studies programmes today.

Chapter VII of the United Nations Charter.

A controversial article in the UN Charter which grants the UN Security Council (see below) the power to "determine the existence of any threat to the peace, breach of the peace, or act of aggression" and to take non-military actions such as economic, diplomatic sanctions and if need be military action against aggressor states so as to "restore international peace and security." A hugely empowering clause within the United Nations, it is one of the provisions which make the Security Council so powerful and, in light of potential politicisation, so controversial.

China threat theory.

Refers to the perception that as the People's Republic of China continues to grow economically, it will pose a military threat to its neighbours in the east Asia region, and perhaps eventually the world. Espoused most prominently by US and Japanese officials. China has in turn responded by stating that this equates to propaganda and a smearing campaign, as China has no military goals and is pursuing a "peaceful rise" and that the "China threat" theory is peddled by US and Japanese politicians for domestic election gains. To what degree China will become a threat to world peace is nonetheless a subject of much scholarly debate.

Chinese economic miracle.

Since reforming its economy, the People's Republic of China (PRC) has seen its economy grow by figures around 10% per year consistently. This places it in a position to surpass the US in terms of GDP (see below) in the next two decades, or even less. This has been welcome news in some parts of the world as it indicates a probable shift from what is claimed to be an exploitative global system under US domination. On the other hand, others greet the news as a cautionary tale as it indicates that as China grows, soon she may be in a position to surpass the US and North Atlantic Treaty Organization militarily and thereby become aggressive towards the rest of the world.

Chomsky, Noam.

Highly acclaimed American linguist, public intellectual and activist, he is a staunch critic of US foreign policy; characterising it as aggressive and ultimately dangerous to world security and to the US itself. Shunned by most of the media establishment, he has used the alternative press and numerous books as an outlet for his criticism. Some of his most influential works include *Public Intellectuals and the New Mandarins* (on the moral obligation of the educated to voice protest against the Vietnam War), *The Fatal Triangle* (on US involvement in the Palestinian question; see below) and *Who Rules the World?*

Clash of civilisations hypothesis.

Refers to the hypothesis articulated by US historian and political scientist Samuel P. Huntington in the early 1990s following the end of the Cold War (see below) in response to Francis Fukuyama's 'end of history' hypothesis (see below). According to the hypothesis, unlike the 20th century Cold War, the post-Cold War 21st century would be characterised not by a clash over ideologies espoused by various states, but would be characterised by violence over culture. Especially noteworthy in Huntington's thesis was the possibility of a clash between western and Islamic civilisations. The events of 9/11 (see above) are argued by some to have vindicated Huntington's hypothesis, while still others argue that the incident and similar subsequent acts of terrorism are lone acts not conducted by a whole civilisation as Huntington hypothesised, but by organisations which are themselves usually deemed to be rogue extremists by individuals within that civilisation itself. It is an important piece of recent International Relations scholarship as its arguments are still being studied and debated.

Clausula rebus sic stantibus.

A principle of international law (see below), it stipulates that a state can revoke its entry into a treaty (see below) if there is a fundamental and unforeseeable change in the circumstances under which it was signed.

Climate change.

Refers to the gradual and sometimes rapid transformation on the earth's general climatic patterns. Throughout its millions of years of existence, the planet has undergone various cycles of climate change that have resulted in various biological outcomes. Scientific consensus today, though there is a minority of scientists who dissent for various reasons, states that the earth is once more experiencing climate change with the earth's temperature incrementally heating due to greenhouse emissions from large-scale industrial activity trapping the sun's rays and thereby making the planet heat up. A controversial topic, government responses to the phenomenon have been varied; ranging from denialism to tabling the issue and making it a part of their policies. A recent milestone in acting against climate change has been the Paris Agreement (see below) reached and signed by 194 governments within the auspices of the United Nations (see below).

Coalition.

A formal or informal grouping of independent states to co-operate with regards to a particular international relations objective. An example is the coalition formed by the US, Britain, Australia and 45 other states to invade Iraq in 2003.

Coalition of the willing.

A term used to refer to the 48 states who agreed to participate in the US-led invasion of Iraq in 2003 while most of the international community condemned the invasion either as unwarranted or as a breach of international procedure. The US, Australia and Poland provided military troops to carry out the invasion, while the rest of the coalition provided logistical support following the invasion.

Cold War.

Lasting roughly from the late 1940s to 1989, it was an ideological and economic conflict between the Soviet Union and the United States. While never seeing actual military confrontation between the two superpowers, it did however see their allies engage in "proxy wars" such as in the Korean Civil War (1950-1953), the South African border wars with its newly independent neighbours. It also saw the invasion by the superpowers of countries deemed to be susceptible to influence by the other, examples include the Vietnam War, and in turn the invasion of Afghanistan by the Soviet Union. It shaped the international era and its consequences are still being weighed to this day.

Colonialism.

Generally, colonialism is the act of one country taking over another's territory and subjugating its peoples. While it is an old practice through which various empires of the past (e.g., the Greek, Roman, Persian, Malian, Nubian and Inca empires) were built, that of Africa and Asia by the European powers (Belgium, Britain, and newly united German Empire), is the most recent and with the most complex legacies, with some arguing that it is still taking place through other, non-direct means such as humanitarian intervention (see below), tariffs (see below) and conditional lending and foreign aid (see below).

Collective Security Treaty Organization (CSTO).

Established in 1992, the Collective Security Treaty Organization is a formal military alliance between 6 eastern European member states (Russia, Armenia, Kazakhstan, Kyrgyzstan, Tajikistan, and Uzbekistan), the organisation is an observer in the United Nations General Assembly (see below). Like the North Atlantic Treaty Organization (NATO; see below), the CSTO is chartered to take collective military action against any aggressor who attacks fellow members. Russia has veto power over establishment of foreign military bases on the territories of CSTO member-states. The CSTO has not yet had a military deployment; Belarusian President Alexander Lukashenko being very critical of CSTO inaction when the President of Kyrgyzstan was ousted in 2010 following protests in that country.

Common market.

A multistate agreement to not only remove trade restrictions such as tariffs (see below) and quotas (see below) and adopt a common external tariff (see customs union) but to also allow a mutual free movement of labour and physical capital among the member states.

Common Security and Defence Policy (CSDP).

Previously called the European Security and Defence Policy, it is one of the key components of the Common Foreign and Security Policy of the European Union (see below). It is responsible for the collective defence and crisis management of countries in the European Union, and unlike the North Atlantic Treaty Organization (see below), is under exclusive and complete EU control and has as its members some countries that are not a part of NATO. Previous deployments include Macedonia in 2003 and the Democratic Republic of the Congo in the same year, under a special resolution from the United Nations Security Council (see below).

Comparative advantage. Also referred to as a niche market, it refers to an inherent advantage that each state is said to have in relation to a particular good or service. Thus, according to economists who adhere to this principle, mainly in the liberal school of thought (see below), a state can grow and maintain its economy through specialising and refining its comparative advantage. Articulated by nineteenth century British economist David Ricardo to defend the principle of free trade, it became a cornerstone of liberal scholars and policymakers. See also international specialisation of labour, World Trade Organization (WTO).

Containment.

A multi-pronged strategy of preventing a perceived threat from acting aggressively against a state or its allies. It is adopted in order to avoid a full-scale confrontation from occurring in the first place. Adopted by the US towards the Soviet Union prior to 1963 through the placement of nuclear weapons in allied countries geographically close to the Soviet Union.

Constructivism.

This is the theory of international relations which argues that the world is in the mind and not an objective reality as the Realists persist. Adherents argue that the world is essentially a set of fictions which statesmen, scholars and general populations agree on. For example, while the physical territory of Eastern Europe is the same, the entity which was once called the Soviet Union was dissolved and so the territories were renamed and with that the attitudes, and perception of the area on the map.

Consulate. An official foreign office of another state within another; its responsibilities generally include issues pertaining to visas and passports as well as import/export licences by those from the consul's home state. Its chief administrator, who has diplomatic immunity (see below), is known as the consul.

Core states. Refers to states which are considered part of the global elite in economic, political and military terms whose wealth is argued by adherents of World systems theory (see below) to have been gained and continues to be maintained through exploitation of the periphery states (see below). States understood to be in this category include the US, Canada, west Europe, Japan and Australia, as well as Israel and South Korea in some scholars' works. See also peripheral states, semi-peripheral states.

Cosmopolitanism.

A broad term referring to the confluence and coexistence between various cultures, philosophies and values in an era of globalisation (see below).

Council of Europe.

A European 47-member international organisation that was established in 1949 to promote human rights, and democracy in the continent. With the exception of Belarus, Kazakhstan and the Vatican City-state, all European states are members of the Council of Europe. Its constituent bodies include the European Court of Human Rights, the Parliamentary Assembly and the Congress of the Council of Europe. The Council of Europe cannot make enforceable laws but may enforce some international agreements that are reached by its member states. No European Union member-state thus far has ever reached EU membership without first being a member of the Council of Europe.

Council on Foreign Relations (CFR).

US trade and foreign policy think tank, it advocates liberalism (see below) with regards to international trade. Thus it also advocates the bolstering of free trade blocs. A reputable organisation established in 1921, it has produced from its alumni various US foreign policymakers, such as former US Secretary of State Henry Kissinger (see below). Headquarters are based in New York City. See http://www.cfr.org/

Counter-hegemony.

A process of defying and challenging the established hegemon (see below). Articulated by Antonio Gramsci (see below).

Cuban embargo.

In 1960, following the rise of socialist Fidel Castro as Prime Minister and his nationalisation of US enterprise operations in the island nation, the US posed an embargo on trade with Cuba with food and medicine as an exception. Two years later, the embargo prevented trade with Cuba altogether. In a 2014 United Nations General Assembly vote to condemn the embargo as a violation of the UN Charter, 188 out of 193 states voted to condemn the embargo; the only two states to make a vote to the contrary were the US and Israel. But beginning in 2015, US President Barack Obama began a process of reversing the embargo through negotiations with the national leadership of Cuba, by then formally led by Raul Castro, Fidel Castro's younger brother.

Customs union.

An agreement between two or more states to trade goods freely with one another with no restrictions (see free trade agreement), and, in addition, to have common tariff and quota rates towards states that are outside of their pact. Examples include the Southern African Customs Union (which is the oldest in the world; see below), and the European Union (see below).

Credit ratings agency.

An entity which assesses a state's ability to repay its debtor (i.e., its creditworthiness), and how much of a risky investment it is on a given ordinal scale. Some of the most reputable ratings agencies are Moody's, Standards and Poor and Fitch.

Crusades, 1095-c.1390.

A series of European-launched invasions on the territories conquered by Muslim rulers in eastern Europe and the Middle East, it was initiated by the Catholic Church in the person of Pope Urban II and was endorsed by numerous kings and nobles. Defined by their participants as a "holy war", the crusades saw wars which claimed thousands of lives, though exact figures are difficult to ascertain. A heated confrontation, it is sometimes taken to be the most explicit kindling of the so-called east-west divide as characterised by the sometimes abrasive relations between Christianised and now secular west and the Muslim east.

Cyberwarfare.

Refers to the use of computer technology to attack, disrupt or unlawfully access another state's computer networks, which, with the advent of digitalisation, are important components to domestic service provision and can contain sensitive information that can be misused once in enemy hands.

Dd

Darfur massacre.

A 2005 incident in Darfur, Sudan in which over 300,000 non-Arabic citizens were killed, allegedly by government and government-allied forces in an attempt to carry out genocide (see below) against them. It sparked international action, and Sudanese President Omar al-Bashir was subsequently placed on the International Criminal Court's wanted list for war crimes and crimes against humanity.

Debt to GDP ratio.

Refers to the proportion of a state's annual revenue, or gross domestic product (GDP; see below), measured against its total debt. Thus a state which has a GDP of $700-billion and debt levels of $350-billion in a given year has a total debt to GDP ratio of 1:2 for that year. As many states are presently in debt (so many states in the world are in debt that less than 5 can be said to be absolutely debt-free), having a high debt to GDP ratio need not mean default by the state because many indebted states remain functional (the US, for example, is the world's largest economy but has a debt level of close to $20-trillion) and even grow while having a high debt to GDP ratio, but it also implies that the state has structural issues within the economy that need addressing.

Defensive realism.

A branch of the Realist school of thought which argues that the state is principally concerned with ensuring its own security and that the general anarchy (see above) in the international arena encourages states to pursue defensive, rather than offensive, security and foreign policies. See also English school.

Deontology.

A moral philosophy according to which acts are good or bad in themselves; articulated by Immanuel Kant (see below).

Dependency theory.

A theory within the Marxist school of thought which argues that resources tend to flow from a "periphery" set of states, nominally identified as Latin America, Africa, Asia and Eastern Europe, to a "core" (see above) set of states, nominally identified as the US, Japan and western Europe, who then enrich themselves through these resources at the expense of the peripheral states. Therefore, proponents of the theory argue, the poor peripheral states are actively underdeveloped by their wealthier counterparts.

Détente.

A period between the early 1970s and 1980 during which the Cold War (see above) was characterised by less strain and the opening up of relations between the superpower adversaries, the United States and the Soviet Union. It came to an end when the Soviet Union invaded Afghanistan between 1979 and 1980.

Diplomacy.

Official recognition and engagement between states. It also refers to the pursuit of settling differences through communication and dialogue as opposed to military engagement.

Diplomatic immunity.

Refers to the rights of a diplomat to not be liable to the laws of the country to whom they represent their home state. A concept that has been practiced for centuries, if not millennia, it is a primary example of customary international law (see below).

Does the Elephant Dance?

A 2011 book by Canadian diplomat and UN official, David M. Malone. It analyses key features, and evolution, of the Indian foreign policy since independence from Great Britain in 1947 to the present and ordains India's growing importance to mean that it will become one of the key superpowers within the first half of this century.

Doctors Without Borders.

Established in 1971, Doctors Without Borders is a Switzerland-based humanitarian organisation that provides immediate medical relief to impoverished, war-ravaged or climate disaster-affected communities to countries worldwide.

Doha Development Round.

An ongoing set of World Trade Organization (see belo) negotiations meant to realise free trade; they commenced in 2001 in Doha, Qatar. One of the major causes of stalemate is the issue of whether agricultural produce should be subject to unrestricted trade; with the European Union, the United States and Japan maintaining subsidies for their domestic agricultural producers and thereby creating barriers to external states who cannot compete effectively with the government-sponsored producers.

Drone attacks in Yemen.

A NATO (see below) remote drone striking campaign that began in 2002 as part of the ongoing

War on Terror (see below); heavily criticised for its indiscriminate killing of combatants and civilians alike. Over 100 unarmed civilians of Yemen are estimated to have been killed by the strikes since the campaign began.

Dutch disease.

Refers to the tendency of states to focus on a newly discovered natural resource market at the expense of industrial and agricultural development, with the outcome that the country becomes almost dependent on that particular mineral and becomes at risk of financial ruin if the price of that resource drops in the volatile market. Derived from the decline in the manufacturing sector in the Netherlands which took place following the discovery of natural gas in 1959.

Ee

e-International Relations (e-IR).

A student-ran journal and publishing house based in the United Kingdom. Focusing mainly on international relations, it publishes and distributes its content for no fees or charges from the readers. See http://e-ir.org/

East African Community (EAC).

A common market originally composed of Kenya, Tanzania and Uganda established in 1967 but later went on to include Burundi, Rwanda and South Sudan once re-established, having been dissolved in 1977. It is a common market arrangement (see above) between the members and there have been plans for the establishment of a single 'East African Federation'.

Ebola epidemic, 2013-2016.

The outbreak of the Ebola virus in West Africa which first appeared in Guinea and later spread to neighbouring Liberia and Guinea and saw minor outbreaks in Nigeria and Mali, as well as the United States. Approximately 28,600 people were infected in one stage or another in the three-year period; and over 11,300 lives were claimed by the outbreak according to figures issued by organisations and governments in the region. Efforts by the World

Health Organization (see below) helped in bringing the situation under control and brought the needed medical resources to alleviate those who had been infected along with their communities. Studies on how the virus spread so rapidly established the causes as rooted in delayed government response and inadequate healthcare systems as well as privatised medical care in countries with low income levels. That this was the outcome of World Bank (see below) and International Monetary Fund (see below) structural adjustment programmes (see below) has been suggested as in the 1980s some states in the region privatised, closed down or scaled back their spending on healthcare infrastructure as that was said to be a drawback to development by the World Bank report written up by Elliot Berg as a condition for borrowing.

Economic Community of West African States (ECOWAS).

A regional grouping of 15 west African states. Established in 1975 its foundational goals include the promotion of economic cooperation in the region as well as "collective self-sufficiency" as well as stability in the region. Composed of the ECOWAS Commission and the ECOWAS Bank for Investment and Development. According to 2013 documents released by former NSA agent Edward

Snowden, ECOWAS had been under US and British surveillance.

Embargo.

Refers to the limiting or elimination of trade with one or more states with the aims usually being rooted in political conflict. Contemporary examples include the embargo imposed by the US on Cuba, as well as by the United Nations (see below) on North Korea (see below). Some states give-in to embargoes and change the behaviour which led to the sanctions in the first place; an example of this is apartheid South Africa which ended minority rule in large part due to the important role played by international embargoes. Still others attempt to overcome the effects of embargoes by adjusting their domestic economy into somewhat self-sufficient ones; an example of such a state is North Korea. See also Cuban embargo.

Embedded liberalism.

Refers to the Keynesian (see below) coexistence of free trade and welfare provision by western states. As these two ideals partially conflict in that the former argues for less state involvement, while the latter advocates for it, such a compromise was unique and important. The system of embedded liberalism persisted from the 1940s to the 1970s when it gained much criticism and in Britain and later the US, in 1980, leaders were elected whose avowed aims were to "roll back" much of the welfare in their respective countries. Nevertheless, embedded liberalism persists in some variations upon some revival after the late 2000s Great Recession (see below).

Emissary.

An individual representing his or her country's government in another state. See also diplomacy.

End of history.

Refers to a hypothesis that predicted that the end of the Cold War (see above) marked the absolute victory for western liberalism and democracy, which was so resounding that there would be no further serious opposition of the sort seen during the latter half of the 20th century. Articulated by US scholar and Harvard University professor Francis Fukuyama in a book titled *The End of History and the Last Man* published in 1992. The events of 9/11 (see above) and subsequent acts of terrorism, the rise of China and Russia and their apparent adversary stances towards the US are seen by some to have greatly discredited Fukuyama's thesis. Nevertheless, it continues to have considerable support from scholars who argue that Fukuyama's central idea was misunderstood in that it did not imply the end of conflict, but the teleological triumph of liberal democracy. Samuel P. Huntington proposed the 'clash of civilisations' hypothesis (see above) as a repost against Fukuyama's end of history hypothesis. See also liberal democratic peace thesis.

English school of thought.

A sub-variant of realism which argues that although there is anarchy in international relations, this could be characterised more as a "society of states" with certain discernible rules, norms and systems which arise out of a collective fear of unrestricted violence shared by all states.

European Central Bank (ECB).

Based in Frankfurt, Germany, the European Central Bank is jointly owned by all 28 central banks of European Union (see below) member states and was established in 1998. Its principal objective is price stability within states that use the Euro (€). The bank, which is in charge of European Union monetary policy (though not fiscal policy; see below), has exclusive control over printing of Euro banknotes, while euro coins may be printed by the various states in the Eurozone upon consent from the ECB.

European Union (EU).

With a lineage dating back to 1958 (or even earlier to 1951 with the formation of the European Coal and Steel Community), with the Treaty of Rome, the European Union is a complex political and economic union of 28 European states. Originally founded by six European states as the European Economic Community (EEC), the EU came to include more states (who fulfilled the entry criteria including democratisation and certain economic reforms) and assumed more rights, responsibilities and mandates such as law-making for member-states, collective European self-defence (see Common Security and Defence Policy above) and economic policy (with a central bank and common currency used by most of its members, the *euro* [€], amongst others). The EU is composed of 7 main arms; the European Council, the Council of the European Union, the European Parliament, the European Commission, the Court of Justice, the European Court of Auditors and the European Central Bank (see above). The subject of controversy and criticism, the union has experienced increasing pushback from within some of its member states. This movement, known as Euroscepticism (see below), gained a major victory with Brexit (see above) in 2016.

Euroscepticism.

This is the name given to the movement which has been continually pushing for the reversal of EU policies and even the shutdown of the EU itself. A continent-wide movement, examples of some its adherents include the United Kingdom Independence Party (UKIP), Alternative for Germany, Golden Dawn (in Greece) and many others, most of whom are under the umbrella of continent-wide allied parties such as the European Conservatives and Reformists (ECR), Europe of Nations and Freedom and the European Alliance for Freedom. Some of its most prominent leaders include Boris Johnson (see below), Nigel Farage of Britain, Marine Le Pen of France, as well as Geert Wilders and Marcel la Graaff of the Netherlands. An increasingly growing tide within the European scene, a recent success for the movement has been the referendum among British people for their country to exit the European Union (see Brexit). Adherents of Euroscepticism point to a variety of supposed defects of the European Union – among these are the inability to regulate immigration (especially in the wake of the Syrian crisis; see below), an alleged power of the European Union to override local jurisdictions that undermine the member nation states and sometimes democracy and self-determination by the local as the European Union can make laws that cannot be easily reversed (if at all) by those who have been elected to govern their countries, too much bureaucracy, expensiveness of membership paid with funds that could possibly be used elsewhere, and restriction on trading abilities of some the nations as they cannot have trade agreements outside the mechanism of the European Union (see customs union) all of which are blamed for the decline in economic living standard in European countries.

Eurozone.

Refers to the union formed by 19 states who adopted the euro (€) as their official currency beginning in 1999. As part of being in the Eurozone, member-states also accede to having their monetary policy set at a collective level by the European Central Bank (see above) in which they each have a representative. The sustainability of such a mechanism has been questioned ever since it was brought into existence; with some raising serious economic and political debate around issues of the potential for contagion in times of crisis and the practicality of integrating states with weak economies with those that have strong economies. The European Central Bank's facilitation of peer-reviewing of budgets has been also seen as increasingly encroaching on what should otherwise be domestic territory of the state and not an outside body.

Extraterritoriality.

Refers to the condition of being made exempt from the laws of the state one is in. It is an example of customary international law (see below). Heads of state as well as diplomats and some multinational corporations (see below) with bilateral investment treaties (see above) so stipulating operate under extraterritoriality. See also diplomatic immunity.

Ff

Failed state.

A controversial term, it refers to a state which is deemed to not be effective at asserting itself upon its territory and may thereby have little to no legitimacy among its citizenry. Various research organisations maintain and publish regular databases of states in accordance with their standing regarding the failed state paradigm. Critics of this paradigm argue that it is a problematic concept due to its criteria being based on notions sometimes deemed unique to some but not all states. See also statehood.

Fanon, Frantz.

Born in French-colonised Martinique, he was a trained psychiatrist who was arguably the most influential anticolonial and postcolonial intellectual of his generation. Supporting the Algerian war of liberation against France, he also wrote a number of works which are still taught and studied in most Postcolonialism studies programmes. In his works he wrote that colonialism was necessarily violent and that, therefore, violence was the only appropriate response in the efforts to throw it off. He also warned of a neo-colonialism (see below) that he saw as inevitable due to the very nature of colonialism which rendered colonies virtually entirely reliant on their colonisers and the continued interest in their former colonies by the former 'mother countries' which linked up with a willingness to cooperate by the new and incoming postcolonial ruling class. His most popular works include *The Wretched of the Earth* (1952), *Black Skin, White Masks* (1959).

FIFA (Fédération Internationale de Football Association).

Established in 1903 to oversee competition among member associations, it is currently the largest such organisation being composed of 211 national football, handball, and beach soccer associations. Since 1930, it has continuously organised the FIFA World Cup, and since 1991 the FIFA Women's World Cup.

Fiscal policy.

Refers to a national, or in the case of the EU (see above) supranational, government's mechanism to influence the economy by setting the tax rates and government spending levels.

Food security.

Refers to the distinguishable access of individuals to healthy, consumable food, and in ways that are concurrent with their human dignity. A primary concern of many governments and intergovernmental organisations as well as their non-governmental counterparts, the guaranteed access to food led to the articulation of the right to food (see below) within the auspices of the United Nations.

Foreign Affairs magazine.

An outlet of the Council on Foreign Relations (see above), a US-based think tank, this magazine regularly publishes articles and reports on international affairs: see http://www.foreignaffairs.com/

Foreign aid.

The act of granting financial, infrastructural donations to a state deemed to be in need of them. It takes many forms, such as short-term disaster relief or the longer-term oriented developmental aid. It has been criticised by some economists and international relations scholars (most notably Dambisa Moyo; see below) for not doing much to assist those it is ostensibly designed to assist through actually flowing back to the donor countries (e.g., through salaries for aid agency employees) and being tied to too many conditions which may work to the benefit of the donor but to the detriment of the recipient state.

Foreign policy.

A given state's general outlook and behaviour towards other states and international institutions. Nominally driven by a particular set of interests.

Forum on China-Africa Relations (FOCAC).

Established in 2000, it serves as a semi-annual summit in which African ministers, diplomats and heads of states engage with the ministers, diplomats and head of state of the People's Republic of China. One of the ongoing trends within FOCAC has been the pledging of large financial, educational and infrastructural donations to Africa by China within an outlined upcoming timetable, and trade commitments and prospects by both sides. The Forum's importance derives from the China-benefitting imbalances in trade between Africa and China, China's excessive focus on raw minerals for export out of Africa and cheap manufactured goods for import into Africa. See also, Beijing consensus.

Free trade agreement (FTA).

An agreement between two states, or a larger group of states, to remove all tariffs (see below), quotas (see below) or any other form of trade restriction, on one another's goods. See also customs union.

Free world.

A controversial designation of states deemed to be open and democratic states as opposed to those deemed to be undemocratic and characterised by a lack of, or insufficient, openness.

"Freedom fries."

Name used to refer to French fries in the US House of Representatives and White House during the presidency of George Bush after the French nation refused to enter into the US-led coalition that invaded Iraq in 2003 when it was alleged (and later discredited) that the Middle Eastern country had been sponsoring the terrorist organisation al-Qaeda (responsible for the 9/11 attacks in New York; see above), and had in its possession weapons of mass destruction and thereby posed a security threat to the US.

Fund for Peace (FFP).

Established in 1957, the Fund for Peace's foundational purpose is peace-aimed research and education. It issues an annual report on fragile states (see above). See http://fragilestatesindex.org/

Fungible resources.

Any good which can be traded or substituted for another; in essence, a commodity.

Gg

Gallup, Inc.

A US-based research company established in 1935. It is mostly known for its public opinion polls which are often regarded as accurate and reliable indicators of domestic and international public opinion.

Game theory.

A branch of study within Behavioural Economics that attempts to predict individual human and group behaviour. Its models have applications for international relations, where they are used to attempt to understand and predict the behaviours of states and international institutions. An example of a game theory scenario is Prisoner's Dilemma (see below).

Gastro-diplomacy.

Refers to the usage of food as a tourism and diplomatic tool to acclimate foreign citizens and leaders towards a particular state.

General Agreement on Tariffs and Trade (GATT).

Formulated in 1947 within the auspices of the United Nations (see below), the General Agreement on Tariffs and Trade was a multilateral trade agreement for the lowering of tariffs (see below) between states. Having gained some 123 signatures by the time of the conclusion of the Uruguay Round (see below), in 1994 it was incorporated into the rationale and framework of the World Trade Organization (see below) established in 1994.

Genocide.

Also known as ethnic cleansing, it is the act of eliminating members of a particular ethnicity within a particular state in order to rid of its members. Debate exists over the question of what criteria, especially in terms of quantity, characterises a scenario as genocidal. The United Nations (see below) prohibits acts of genocide and is obligated to act in order to prevent or remedy genocidal situations principally through the United Nations Security Council (see below) and the International Court of Justice (see below).

Geneva Conventions.

A set of voluntary rules, guidelines and protocols that relate to the humane conduct of war. Crafted and refined in conferences taking place in Geneva in 1864, 1906, 1929 and 1945. Its focus points include the rights of prisoners of war (POWs), the wounded and sick and unarmed civilians.

Global democracy.

A broad term generally referring to the global population's ability to influence the decision making processes and institutions whose decisions impact them.

Global governance.

In absence of a "world government", this is the regulatory framework brought about by the set of voluntary international institutions, mechanisms, norms, values, agreements and procedures which most states in the international system abide by. This can range from trade (mediated by the World Trade Organisation), conduct in war (guided by the Geneva Conventions), and justice (imposed by the International Criminal Court) amongst others.

Globalisation.

A broad term referring to the increasing state of interconnectedness that has arose in the previous century due to innovations and intensification in financial flows, travel, technology and communications, and popular culture. Scholars differ on their assessment of what globalisation means for the centrality of the state as the principal agent of international relations, with some arguing that the state is increasingly becoming irrelevant as borders become less significant due to multinational corporations (see below), international organisations, and events challenging the state's ability to regulate the general trends of international proportion. Some on the other hand, especially Realists (see below), argue that the state remains the principal agent of international relations as incidents happen through state-mandated policies. Globalisation is both supported and opposed by some in significant measure. Proponents laud it for its supposed capacity to encourage collaboration, free trade, as well as cosmopolitanism (see above). Critics point to its supposedly negative effects on the environment, national identity and national economies. See also the G8, the Great Recession.

Golan Heights.

Refers to a region of Syria partially under Israeli control since 1967, following the Six-Day War. Israel has since the 1980s been building settlements in the region to the effect that many Syrians in the territory have accepted Israeli citizenship. The Israeli government has since the 1970s been stating that it would grant the land back to Syria provided Syria agreed to peace and accompanying conditions, including most recently the severing of ties with Iran. However, Syria has found these terms not agreeable and the emergence of the Syrian civil war (see below) as well as that of ISIS (see below) have further diminished chances of the territory being reverted into Syrian government control. A strip between the two parts controlled by the two states has been under United Nations demilitarised control since 1974.

Government-in-exile.

Refers to a group of individuals making claim to being the legitimate government of a state, but otherwise unable to practice their rule over the territory due to domestic pressures or otherwise, and forced to reside in a foreign state. Governments-in-exile may or may not receive recognition from other governments, and thereby strengthen or weaken their cause accordingly. Historical examples include the Free French government during the Second World War which was forced to reside in Britain while their home country was overrun and occupied in 1940 by Nazi Germany who set-up a puppet regime ran by French officials who collaborated or at least capitulated to Germany. Present-day examples include the Dalai Lama, who is recognised by some as the legitimate head of Tibet and resides in India due to pressures from the People's Republic of China's government which has official control of that region.

Gramsci, Antonio.

Italian Marxist (see below) and critic of the dictatorial Fascist regime under Benito Mussolini, he wrote a set of essays and journal entries which were published after his death as *Prison Notebooks*. According to Canadian labour activist and theoretician, Robert Cox, this work was the first explicit application of Marxist theory into international affairs as it detailed how rich, but few states, are able to coerce the poor, but numerous states. According to Gramsci, just as the few wealthy citizens in most states are able to repel the revolutionary sentiments among the poor through narratives which justify the hierarchy, the wealthy states subdue the poor states without resorting to violence by weaving narratives which justify the hierarchy and exploitation. This he labelled 'hegemony' (see below).

Great Recession, 2007-9.

The international financial crisis which followed the bursting of the US housing market's bubble following reckless lending by banks and poor regulation of the financial market by governments. The collapse led a worldwide recession as well as high job losses, and, for the first time in over thirty years, a negative international growth rate in 2008.

The crisis was alleviated by increased government spending in major countries accompanied with a decrease in interest rates so that people would be willing and able to purchase goods and services and thereby reduce the level of unemployment.

Greek debt crisis.

Beginning after the Great Recession (see above), the Greek debt crisis was initiated by structural weakness in the Greek economy along with data that was soon made public revealing that the Greek government had hitherto undercounted its debt levels. Greece's credit worthiness was lowered in face of declining investor confidence. So far, the country, which is a European Union (see above) member needed three sets of International Monetary Fund (see above), European Group and European Central Bank (see above) bailouts in 2010, 2012 and 2015; in turn, the government of Greece was required to adopt austerity measures such as increasing the retirement age, cutting government spending on some social services, enacting tax hikes, and even an ATM withdrawal limit of €60 for some time in 2015. Amidst a serious recession, widespread unemployment, and rising homelessness among Greeks, the austerity measures have been widely unpopular and have seen a rise in right-wing,

Eurosceptic (see above) sentiments as seen with the Golden Dawn nationalist movement.

Green Revolution.

Refers to the spread of agricultural technologies and methods to developing countries in the decades following the end of the Second World War that saw increases in agricultural produce and billions of people saved from potential starvation. The technological proliferation, taking place most notably in the 1960s and 1970s, was initiated by US biologist Norman Borlaug who received the Nobel Peace Prize in 1970.

Greenpeace.

Established in 1969, it is a controversial international climate advocacy group with a membership of over 15,000 people, active in over 40 countries, it is one of the largest such organisations in the world. A consultative member of the United Nations Economic and Social Council (see below).

Gross domestic product (GDP).

The total amount of goods and services produced domestically within a country in a particular year in financial terms. It is distinct from gross national product (GNP; see below).

Gross national product (GNP).

The financial measure of the total amounts of goods and services produced by citizens and corporations of a certain state, including those produced from outside the territory of that given state.

Group of 77 (G77).

Formed in 1964 by 77 developing states within the United Nations (see below) as a coalition for bargaining and forwarding their collective interests, the G77 presently consists of 134 member-states. A major force in the international anti-apartheid movement, it has also been a major force behind disarmament. The G77 has however been criticised of not taking firmer action against climate change which it has not prioritised due to the claim that the bulk of its members are still developing states for whom environmentalism would supposedly counteract their industrialisation path.

Group of Eight (G8).

Established in 1971, the G8 is a coalition of the eight most developed nations in the world; Britain, Canada, France, Germany, Italy, Japan, Russia (included in 1998), and the United States. The G8's annual meeting acts as a forum on the major issues confronting the world; former issues have included international financial regulation, the climate, and poverty. In 2014, following its annexation of Crimea, Russia was suspended and fellow members posed economic sanctions on it.

Group of Twenty (G20).

Formed in 1999, the G20 is a forum composed of 19 leaders and central bank governors of 19 leading economies as well as representatives from the European Union. Its foundational aim is the promotion of international financial stability. Aggregated, the GDPs of the G20 members total more than 80% of international trade. The forum has met every year since 2009 but has increasingly seen major protests erupt around its summits due to anti-globalisation, anti-capitalist and anti-establishment sentiments, especially since the Great Recession (see above).

Guantanamo Bay detention camp.

US-owned and operated military detention camp in Guantanamo Bay in Cuba. The prison was established under the presidency of George W. Bush in 2002 to hold and question suspects of terrorism indefinitely (for as long as deemed necessary) without trial as part of the war on terror (see below); it quickly became the centre of controversy as inmates were said to be subjected to torture under the name of "enhanced interrogation techniques" by the US Navy and reports of inmate suicide surfaced. A pledge by President Barack Obama to close down the facility, which is criticised by many organisations and countries worldwide as well as within the US itself for human rights violations, did not materialise.

Gunboat diplomacy.

Phrase used to describe a form of international engagement that is characterised by general negotiation but with the imminent threat of military attack made clear. Best captured in the African proverb that the 26th President of the United States, Theodore Roosevelt, was fond of quoting: "speak softly but carry a big stick." Scholars such as Noam Chomsky (see above), Gore Vidal (see below) and Edward Said have claimed that this characterises US post-World War II foreign policy, and some to even earlier times, such as the late nineteenth century when the US virtually colonised Cuba, Guam, Hawaii, the Philippines, and Puerto Rico.

Hh

Haitian pig scandal, 1981.

The creole pig species was unique to Haiti, where it was a significant part of the rural economy – it was relatively easy to maintain, the droppings from the pigs could be used to fertilise the coffee crops which could then be sold for profit. In the early 1980s, an African swine fever epidemic broke out in neighbouring Dominican Republic. There was a fear among US officials in the United States Agency for International Development (USAID; see below) that the disease would spread to Haiti and then the US where it would hurt US agriculture. All the pigs in Haiti were executed by US officials by permission from the Haitian dictator, driving the species into extinction. The farmers were compensated with Iowa pigs imported from the US. These replacements proved difficult to maintain, as they needed expensive feeds. Consequently, the living standards of the already impoverished Haitian rural dwellers declined considerably further.

Hegemonic stability theory.

A complex theory of international relations according to which the existence of a single superpower, or hegemon (see below), results in stability in the international arena because in absence of a "world government" the hegemon makes and, importantly, is able to enforce rules and norms through the use of diplomacy and if need be the threat of force.

Hegemony.

A single country's dominance of the international arena. Can also be used to define a state's dominance within its region; such a state is said to be a regional hegemon. Though there is no scholarly consensus on what constitutes a hegemon, military and economic preponderance are general indicators. See also unipolar international order.

Heritage Foundation.

American conservative think-tank, it analyses both domestic US and international affairs. The Heritage Foundation produces reports on contemporary issues with a Realist and at times Eurosceptic (see above) perspective, and usually makes testimonies before the US Congress (see below) wherein they nominally argue for a hard line against any perceived threats to US national interest.

Holy Roman Empire.

Deemed "neither Holy, nor Roman, nor an Empire" by French 17th century *philosophe* Voltaire, this was the entity which lasted from 800AD to 1806 when

Napoleon Bonaparte (see below) dissolved it through the Treaty of Pressburg and created the puppet regime he named Confederation of the Rhine which was composed of the same states, except Austria and Westphalia (on whose throne he placed his youngest brother, Jerome Bonaparte). It was a collection of over 300 virtually independent north Italian and German-speaking states in present-day Germany that was ruled by an elected Emperor confirmed by the Pope to whom he owed allegiance. Composed of what is today Germany and Austria, it was indeed the closest forerunner to the present-day Federal Republic of Germany.

Hoover Institution.

A think tank whose full name is the Hoover Institution on War, Revolution and Peace, it is based in Stanford University in California. Founded in 1919 by future President Herbert Hoover, its main focus is the state of international affairs as they relate to the US, and the spread of an American brand of freedom worldwide. It has been described as nominal conservative, although its board members tend to resist this form of identification.

Horn of Africa.

Refers to the region in east Africa composed of Djibouti, Eritrea, Ethiopia and Somalia.

Human development index (HDI).

Developed by Indian economist and professor, Amartya Sen, and Pakistani economist, Mahbub al Haq, it is a measure of a state's investment in its citizens as measured by education and health as well as individual yearly income per citizen. The United Nations (see below) issues out annual rankings of countries by how much they improved or declined in their human development as measured by the HDI.

Human Rights Watch (HRW).

US-based human rights research and advocacy group established in 1978, the Human Rights Watch opposes what it deems human rights violations such as capital punishment, press censoring, and religion-based suppression amongst others. It makes regular researched publications on violations of human rights which in turn are used to pressure oppressive governments to relinquish the practices.

Humanitarian intervention.

This is the act by a single state, or a coalition of states, of militarily intervening in a country with the view to remove the ruling regime of a state which it deems oppressive to its peoples. Specific criteria for – as well as the legality of – humanitarian intervention are among the most debated topics in international relations today. See also Article VII, sovereignty.

Ii

Iberia.

Refers to Portugal and Spain, the two states which form the Iberian Peninsula, collectively. In broader terms it can mean Portuguese- and Spanish-speaking areas of the world formerly colonised by the two states, especially those in south America.

Imperialism.

The subjugation and imposition of a way of life, as well as extraction of resources belonging to a distinct people for political and economic gain. Scholars differ on the distinction between colonialism (see above) and imperialism, though many scholars state that colonialism may be said to be one of many types of imperialism. See also neo-colonialism.

Import substitution and industrialisation (ISI).

Refers to an economic policy which includes the boosting and forging of domestic industries through increased government subsidisation as well as the imposing of trade restrictions such as quotas (see below) and tariffs (see below) on foreign goods, so as to eliminate reliance on foreign imports. Practitioners and proponents of import substitution and industrialisation often argue that this is necessary for the nurturing and advancing of domestic infant industries as it leads to employment creation and putting an end to the perceived exploitation inflicted by outside states with whom fair terms of trade are deemed impossible. ISI was applied most avowedly in Latin America, and later in some African state, in the decades following the end of the Second World War. The introduction of structural adjustment programmes (see below) in the 1980s by the International Monetary Fund (see below) and the World Bank (see below) meant the virtual abandoning of this policy as some of the pre-conditions for loans were the liberalisation of markets. Import substitution and industrialisation has a number of proponents nonetheless in contemporary times in North Korea (see below) under the name of *juche* which is meant to foster resilience and self-reliance in that East Asian state in the wake of the sanctions placed on it on account of its domestic and foreign policy practices.

Indian Ocean Rim Association (IORA).

Composed of 21 states that border the Indian Ocean, it was established in 1997 as a regional association intended to foster cooperation and closer interaction among member-states. Its member-states straddle three continents: Africa, Asia and Australia. Headquarters are based in Mauritius.

Intergovernmental organisation (IGO).

An organisation whose members are states. Each IGO has its particular aims and terms of membership. Examples include the United Nations (see below), the European Union (see above) and the African Union (see above).

International Atomic Energy Agency (IAEA).

Established in 1957 by the United Nations (see below), it is an international organisation that actively promotes the usage of nuclear energy for non-military applications. Accused of being a virtual lobbyist for nuclear energy companies, and criticised for ineffective responses to the 1986 Chernobyl nuclear disaster in the then Ukrainian Soviet Socialist Republic and the 2011 Fukushima nuclear accident in Japan. Granted the Nobel Peace Prize in 2005.

International Bank for Reconstruction and Development (IBRD).

Formed in 1944 at the Bretton Woods conference, the International Bank is, along with the International Development Association, one of the two organs of the World Bank (see below). It is owned and ran by various states who are shareholders within the bank. Its foundational aim was to assist in rebuilding Europe after its infrastructure was destroyed by World War II (see below). It presently offers loans to states for projects related to education, health, infrastructure, transportation and sanitation.

International Center for the Settlement of Investment Disputes (ICSID).

A World Bank (see below) international arbitration institution which sees to the resolution of disputes related to investments made across states. See also bilateral investment treaty.

International Commission on Intervention and State Sovereignty (ICISS).

2001 temporary commission established by the Canadian government to promulgate the concept of humanitarian intervention (see below) for the sake of spreading democracy as the "responsibility to protect (RtoP; see below).

International Court of Justice (ICJ).

Established in 1945, the International Court of Justice is the main legal arm of the United Nations. Its purpose is to settle legal disputes, and to provide legal counsel on legal questions that stem from the UN General Assembly. Its landmark judgement was its ruling in 1986 that the US's covert war in Nicaragua was a violation to international law. Enhanced as well as limited by its reliance on the UN Security Council for enforcements of judgements whose functions can be vetoed by a single member state in the Security Council.

International Criminal Court (ICC).

Based in The Hague in the Netherlands, the International Criminal Court was established in 1997 through the Rome statute and began functioning in 2002. It is intended to prosecute perpetrators of genocide, crimes against humanity as well as war crimes in conjunction with domestic judiciaries of member states, of which there are some 124. Individuals get tried in the court through three main procedures: referral by the United Nations Security Council (see below), referral by governments and by the discretion of the chief prosecutor of the ICC. States that are not party to the Rome statute may still have their citizens referred to the Court for prosecution. The Court has been criticised of thus far having only tried and prosecuted African individuals. To that effect, in 2016 Burundi, the Gambia and South Africa announced intention to withdraw from the Court.

International Criminal Tribunal for Rwanda (ICTR).

Formed in 1994 by the United Nations Security Council (see below) in the wake of the Rwandan genocide of 1994, it was established to prosecute individuals guilty of committing the genocide. It completed some 50 trials before it was officially closed in 2015. Headquarters were based in Arusha, Tanzania.

International Criminal Tribunal for Yugoslavia (ICTY).

The first international criminal tribunal since the Nuremberg trials, it was formed in 1993 to prosecute individuals guilty of committing acts of genocide and other war crimes during the Balkans' wars of the 1990s. It has thus far prosecuted 160 individuals. Headquarters are based in The Hague, Netherlands.

International Development Association (IDA).

Established in 1960, the International Development Association offers loans below average interest rates to the poorest and impoverished states in the world. Having made loans totalling over US$238-billion, it is the largest such organisation in the world. Along with the International Bank for Reconstruction and

Development (see above), it is part of the World
Bank (see below).

International Labour Organization (ILO).

Established in 1919 as part of the League of Nations
(see below) and later incorporated into the United
Nations in 1946, it is an international labour agency
that seeks to standardise labour practices, and
eliminate discrimination in employment.

International law.

More a label for the general implicit and explicit
norms, principles and voluntary self-regulation and
abiding by treaties than an actual legal system with
power in the domestic sense. It acts as a balancing
force to the so-called anarchy which characterises
international politics; it acts as a benchmark for
behaviour in the international arena. See Geneva
Conventions, global governance, International
Criminal Court, International Court of Justice, the
United Nations.

International political economy.

The study of the interaction and interplay between
politics and economics in the international arena. A
broad sub-field of International Relations, its
practitioners explore various scenarios, theories,

institutions and histories that pertain to international trade, regional integration and foreign aid amongst others.

International Red Cross and Red Crescent Movement.

Formulated in 1863, the Red Cross and Red Crescent Movement is the oldest international medical relief organisation in the world. It provides care to those wounded in conflicts. It has some 97-million volunteers worldwide, and three distinct and independent sub-organisations; the International Committee of the Red Cross, the International Federation of the Red Cross and Red Crescent Societies as well as the various divisions of the National Red Cross and Red Crescent Societies which exist in most countries. It has been awarded the Nobel Peace Prize three different times: in 1917, 1944 and 1963.

International specialisation of labour.

Refers to the apparent compartmentalisation of certain tasks to certain regions and states - capital intensively in the US and western Europe, manufacturing in Asia and natural resource production in Latin America, the Middle East, and Africa.

International Monetary Fund (IMF).

An international financial organisation based in Washington and formulated, along with the World Bank Group and the nascent World Trade Organisation, in the Bretton Woods Conference of 1944. The IMF is primarily a regulatory and financial oversight body with some lending functions and assisted greatly in the rebuilding of war-destroyed Europe. In later years, especially following the 1970s, it began to assume a more powerful role as newly independent African and Asian states were seeking sources of funding and the IMF sought to use its means to apply economic and political reforms in these countries through structural adjustment programmes (see below). The IMF has been a major subject of criticism; with much of this criticism being over its history of funding authoritarian regimes (including apartheid South Africa), its supposedly impractical economic recommendations in some instances, its penchant for intervention and for allegedly causing more harm than good such as the resultant recession in Greece after its intervention starting in 2010.

Interpol.

Formed in 1923, Interpol enhances efforts to investigate and prosecute a wide array of crimes including corruption, genocide (see below), human trafficking and environmental crimes. Headquarters are based in Lyon, France.

Intifada.

Arabic term meaning "uprising." It is used to describe incidences of large-scale violent and non-violent protests by Palestinian (see below) citizens. The first intifada took place between 1987 and 1993 and saw clashes between stone-throwing Palestinians and armed Israeli Defense Forces (IDF) personnel resulted in the death of over 1,162 Palestinians, as well as 100 Israelis and 60 IDF members. It was brought to a conclusion by the Oslo Accords (see below), which ensured concessions for both sides (recognition for Israel by the Palestine Liberation Organization; see below, and international recognition of the Palestine Liberation Organization as the sole representative for Palestinians by many countries as well as a United Nations observer status for the organisation). The second intifada took place from 2000 to 2005 and saw a higher casualty count due to the number of participants and use of suicide bombings and larger deployment of personnel by the IDF; an estimated 3,000 Palestinians and 1,000 Israelis died. The Israeli government ended its occupation of the Gaza strip, but erected the now notorious wall on the West Bank.

Iran nuclear deal.

A deal reached in 2015 with reluctance by the US and Iran for the latter to develop nuclear stations but purely for energy and not military reasons and gives the international community compulsory access to observe the Iranian government in its procedures. It was criticised by many parties, most notably the US Congress (see below) and Israel for practically granting Iran the nuclear bomb and therefore allowing it to pose a bigger threat to Israel, with whom it has prickly relations due to its support for Palestine and even the US with whom it has not had friendly relations since 1979 when the Middle Eastern country underwent a revolution and a pro-American king was overthrown and the (religious) theocratic form of government was established. Supporters of the deal point to its aversion of war between Iran and Israel, its ensuring that Iran develops its nuclear stations under supervision and therefore making it less likely that Iran will build a nuclear bomb (it would not have otherwise been known whether it was a bomb or a power station being built without the deal), and of improving of relations between sanction-ravaged Iran and the rest of the world.

Iron Curtain.

A term used during the Cold War (see above) to refer to the division of Europe between Soviet and US spheres of influence; with the east under communism and the west under capitalism. The cleavage also took organisational terms as western Europe was part of the extant North Atlantic Treaty Organization (see below) and its eastern counterpart was part of the now extinct Warsaw Pact. The term 'Iron curtain' was first used in a speech by Sir Winston Churchill who was by then out of his initial premiership of Britain to warn the US that its Second World War ally, the Soviet Union, could not be trusted for long and that aggression would begin anew as the Soviet Union would seek to dominate and shape global affairs.

Islamic State of Syria and Iraq (ISIS).

Also referred to as the Islamic State of Syria and the Levant (ISIL) or Daesh, it is a terrorist organisation that claims allegiance to Sunni Islam. Its expressed aim is to establish a state ran in accordance with their interpretation of Islamic scriptures. In 2014, the organisation captured large swathes of land in civil war-torn and poorly controlled Iraq and Syria and proclaimed a new caliphate (an Islamic empire). The US and its local rebel allies including the

Kurdish militia Peshmerga have been actively attempting to eliminate the organisation. Its alleged practices have included military conscription, sex trafficking, heavy taxation, deportation or killing of non-Muslims and Muslims that are Shi'ite and not Sunni. ISIS has also successfully and unsuccessfully organised or inspired numerous terrorist attacks in Belgium, France, Germany and other countries.

Isolationism.

A manner of crafting foreign policy (see above) that is characterised by a voluntary self-insulation from world politics; a general lack of engagement with the rest of the world that goes beyond mere neutrality and in fact amounts to a near total silence. Adopted by the US before 1914 in order to avoid "entangling alliances" as articulated by its first President, George Washington.

Jj

Jean, Wyclef. US Haiti-born rapper and philanthropist, he rallied funds for assistance for his birth country following the earthquake that left much of the island country destroyed in 2010 through his Yele Haiti foundation and Hope for Haiti Now telethon; he was later mired in controversy when accusations surfaced that the majority of the funds were not used for humanitarian purposes. He tried to run for President of Haiti in the same year, but could not as he had not been a resident of Haiti for 5 years before the election.

Jim Yong Kim. Korean-American physician and anthropologist, he served as President of Dartmouth College before being appointed President of the World Bank (see below) by US President Barack Obama (see below).

Johnson, Boris. British journalist, author and politician, he has been serving as the Secretary for Foreign Affairs and Commonwealth Relations since July 2016. Campaigning for Britain to exit the European Union (see Brexit; see also European Union), the former Mayor of London is one of the main faces of Euroscepticism in contemporary Britain.

Jolie, Angelina. Prominent Hollywood actress and philanthropist, she has worked extensively with the United Nations (see below) on various campaigns and initiatives that touch on such issues as education, climate change and women's rights. She is also a noted refugee advocate, being the Special Envoy for the United Nations High Commissioner for Refugees.

Kk

Kant, Immanuel.

18th century German philosopher, he spelled out two distinct influential moral and epistemological systems that shaped subsequent European thought. On the international front, he articulated in his 1795 essay 'Perpetual Peace: A Philosophical Sketch' a theory for a worldwide federation, or government, which would bring about eternal peace. He is among the founders of liberalism (see below).

Kashmir.

An Asian territory officially under Indian control but parts of which are claimed by Pakistan and China. There are also a large number of Kashmiri citizens who wish for Kashmir to become an independent state. It has been the main source of tension in Indo-Pak relations as well as between China and India.

Kennedy, John F.

International Relations student at Harvard, and author of *Why England Slept* (a study of British military standing before the Second World War), he was the US President from 1960 until his assassination in 1963. He averted nuclear war with the Soviet Union during the Cuban missile crisis at the height of the Cold War (see below) by agreeing to a US withdrawal of its nuclear weaponry in

Greece and Turkey in exchange for the Soviet Union doing the same in Cuba. Subsequently, his staff proposed a direct line of communication between Washington and Moscow which still stands to this day.

Keynesian economics.

Refers to the set of economic theories brought forth by British economist John Maynard Keynes, according to which economic stability essentially lies in the involvement of government in curtailing the aggregate demand (and therefore employment) to the necessary level through government spending. Thus, according to Keynesian economists, the public and private sectors both have a role to play in preventing economic collapse. Unlike the earlier classical economics that prevailed before the advent of Keynes, he did not see the market as inherently self-correcting and advocated governmental involvement in times of economic slumps. Keynesian economic outlooks were present in the mitigation of the Great Depression in the 1930s, and most recently in the face of the Great Recession of 2007-9 (see above) when governments world over not only undertook various job-creating public works projects and tax-lowering initiatives (to encourage aggregate spending and therefore higher aggregate demand) but also bailed out private corporations from debt, bankruptcy and near total collapse.

Kissinger, Henry.

International relations scholar and diplomat, the German-born Henry Kissinger completed his PhD in Harvard University and later served as the foreign affairs advisor to the United States President Richard Nixon between 1968 and 1974 and later President Gerald Ford between 1974 and 75, he was responsible for the formation of US foreign policy during the Cold War in these years. Controversially pushing for increased US bombing of Vietnam (more than were dropped in the entirety of the Second World War), Cambodia, and Laos and the de facto colonisation of (potentially communist allied) East Timor by ally Indonesia immediately after it gained independence from Portugal in 1970, he also engineered the improvement of US-China relations in 1974. His many publications include *A World Restored: Metternich, Castlereagh and the Problems of Peace, 1812* (1957), *Nuclear Weapons and Foreign Policy* (1957), *On China* (2011) and *World Order* (2014).

Korea-Africa Forum (KAF).

Formed in 2006, KAF is a regular forum in which African ministers and heads of states gather with the South Korean diplomats, ministers and President. To date there have been six of these high-level meetings.

Kremlin. Former royal palace in Moscow, it serves as the Russian seat of government.

Kurdish people.

An ethnic group living in a region spread out into southern Turkey and Syria, northern Iran and Iraq with no independent state of their own, it has over 30 million members; thus the description of them as the world's largest people without a land. They have been subjected to harassment and ill-treatment by the governments of the countries in which they reside, most infamous was an attempt to exterminate them by the Saddam Hussein government of Iraq. Often afflicted by ongoing unrest in the region, some of its members have become members of a majority Kurdish armed force named Peshmerga funded by the US, which has been instrumental in fighting against ISIS (see above).

L1

Lagarde, Christine.

French lawyer, and former French finance minister, she has been the Managing Director of the International Monetary Fund (see above) since 2011. She has controversially overseen the imposition of austerity measures in debt-ravaged Greece by the IMF, and in 2016 refused further funding for the country.

Latin America.

A geopolitical denotation of Portuguese- and Spanish-speaking states in North and South America; historically colonised and settled by people of these states during the years following the discovery of the continent by Christopher Columbus. Many of them later gained independence in the nineteenth century while Spain and Portugal were facing a crisis of their own during Napoleon I of France's expansion (see below).

League of Nations.

A now-defunct body which is nominally seen as the predecessor to the United Nations (see below), this body was formed at the end of the First World War as a brain-child of US President Woodrow Wilson (see below). Having no more than 50 members and with US Congress (see below) having refused to rectify it, it was a toothless organisation that was more useful as a symbolic than legal or military force. Its major projects included the creation of "mandates" in Africa and the Middle East – in essence, this was the transfer of territories (Togo, Tanzania, Namibia, and Senegal in Africa and Syria, Iraq and Iran in the Middle East) from defeated German and Ottoman empires to the victorious British and French. It failed to prevent Italian invasion of Ethiopia, and Japanese invasion of China and was incapable of enforcing the Kellogg-Brand Pact which compelled members to limit their armaments.

Levels of analysis.

A manner of studying foreign policy that involves assessing policy-making from three levels: (1) the individual (usually statesmen and other influential persons that are capable of shaping the foreign policy of a given country); (2) the state; and (3) the international system. Articulated by Kenneth Waltz (see below).

Liberalism.

Also called idealism, it is a theory of international relations which argues that the world *should* be characterised by cooperation, and increased trade.

Adherents argue that increases in trade lead to interconnectedness that makes military confrontation undesirable and virtually too costly to take place.

Liberal-democratic peace thesis.

The term used to describe the lack of any wars between liberal democracies throughout history, it is one of the main points that liberals (see above) use to argue for an adoption of liberal principles on the domestic and international scenes.

Lord's Resistance Army (LRA).

A rebel force led by Joseph Kony who claims to be a prophet, the Lord's Resistance Army has been engaged in a civil war with the Ugandan government, which it seeks to overthrow, since 1987. The LRA has been the subject of much criticism, and has been targeted by Uganda and neighbouring states in the central African region including Sudan, the Central African Republic and the Democratic Republic of the Congo, with assistance from the US, the United Nations, and its encompassing Peacekeeping forces (see below). Tactics used by the LRA have included child soldiers, rape, sex-slavery, abductions and mass murder. Currently, Joseph Kony who is a fugitive from the International

Criminal Court (see above) is believed to be in hiding in South Sudan.

Mm

Malthusian trap.

Refers to the theory brought forth by 18th century British economist Thomas Robert Malthus that argues that there is an inherent inability of the earth's resources to sustain the growing human population. Thus, according to Malthus, various elements such as disease, famine and even war, would act to cut down human population. A controversial theory, to what extent Malthus was correct is hugely engaged with by scholars, officials and organisations today in their own attempts to respond to present-day hunger in the world. Some argue that the technological innovations, as seen for example with the Green revolution (see above) have meant that Malthus' hypothesis has been rendered implausible, while others point to political reasons as the nominal root cause of widespread poverty and famine in the present world. See also food security, right to food.

Mars colonisation project.

An ongoing attempt to place humans on (and perhaps eventually populate and settle) the planet Mars; organisations engaged with the project include SpaceX and NASA (see below).

Marxism.

A theory of international relations which argues that the world is characterised by economic unfairness which is designed by the powerful states at the expense of the poor. Adherents argue that the so-called institutions of international cooperation (such as the UN, WTO and IMF) are nothing but the tools of the powerful to perpetuate their positions of influence.

Merkel, Angela.

German chemist, and Chancellor since 2005. Often called the 'Chancellor of the Free World,' she is one of the most influential figures in European politics. Some of her most important acts include that of imposing, along with the IMF (see above), austerity measures on Greece after that country's debt default following the Great Recession (see above), her pushing for the allowing of entry by Syrian refugees fleeing the civil war in their home-country into EU states, and her handling of the Crimean crisis which took place after the Crimea declared independence from prospective EU member-state Ukraine and subsequent joining of the Russian Federation.

Metternich, Klemens von.

Often referred to as "Europe's Conductor," he was the aristocratic chief diplomat for the monarch of the Austrian Empire, he was responsible for the formation of the alliances, balance of power and international order following the end of the Napoleonic Wars which saw the re-shifting of European borders and the suppression of revolutionary tendencies in Europe. The "Concert of Nations" is the name given to the system he created; it ensured a sustained period of peace never before seen in Europe – lasting a hundred years from 1815 to 1915, it was interrupted by the outbreak of the First World War.

Millennium Development Goals (MDGs).

A set of 8 goals to which all United Nations (see below) member states in 2000 agreed to assist in achieving by the year 2015. These goals were: the eradication of extreme poverty (see below), universal primary school education, ensuring gender equality, reversing climate change (see above), curbing of child mortality, enhancing maternal health, to combat HIV/AIDS and other serious epidemics as well as developing a global partnership for development. The realisation of the goals has been deemed a mixed result with some states achieving many, while others failed to meet even a few. In 2016, the Sustainable Development Goals were launched.

Monetary policy.

Refers to the process by which central banks of states, which are in charge of printing and suppling currency, regulate their monetary supply so as to meet or approximate a particular interest rate. See also monetary policy.

Monroe Doctrine.

Refers to a US foreign policy outlook that was initiated under President James Monroe in 1823 that formed the basis of US relations with Europe and Latin America (see above). According to the doctrine, the old powers of Europe were to no longer interfere or seek to colonise any independent states in Latin America without it being interpreted by the US as an act of aggression towards the US itself. Instead, it was to be a US sphere of influence. As part of the Monroe Doctrine, the US became the dominant power of the American continents; establishing de facto colonies in Cuba, Puerto Rico, installing virtual puppet regimes, fostering government coups and carving a US-ran canal in otherwise sovereign Latin American states. To what extent the Monroe Doctrine is still relevant is the subject of much debate.

Moyo, Dambisa.

Zambian economist and author. Having worked at the World Bank and other international financial services organisations, she became an ardent critic of foreign aid (see above), particularly towards sub-Saharan Africa. In her 2009 book *Dead Aid* she argues that aid is ineffective as it tends to go to countries with corrupt governments who misuse the funds, and huge sums of the aid grants tend to go back to the donor countries through salaries for agency employees, most of whom are from the donor countries. Her other publications include *How the West Was Lost* (2011) and *Winner Take All: China's Race for Resources and What It Means for the World* (2012).

Multinational corporation (MNC).

A corporation which maintains operations in more than one country. Debate exists as to whether they have a positive or negative impact on the domestic economies in which they operate and the international political economy at large.

Multipolar international order.

A global order in which there are three or more dominant states and whose (sometimes conflicting) interests tend to shape world politics.

Mutually assured destruction (MAD).

Alluding to a scenario in which two opposing states, or coalitions, both have nuclear weaponry: due to the great threat posed by even a single nuclear attack by the other, both parties are therefore deemed to be less likely to make the first strike against the other. This has been the ironic relative peace between states with nuclear weapons since nuclear proliferation in the 20th century. Some scholars argue that it explains why there was never actual military confrontation between the US and the Soviet Union, and the stand-off between North Korea and the US in contemporary times.

Nn

Napoleon I of France.

Born on the island of Corsica, then an independent state before invasion by France, he was a military general who later became the political leader of France as its First Consul and then declared himself Emperor. His rule saw a period of wars in which virtually all of Europe (most notably Austria, Britain, Prussia and Russia) were at war with him and his French Empire as part of a coalition, the Allies. These Napoleonic Wars as they are called, saw France acquire Holland, Belgium, Spain, Poland (as the Duchy of Warsaw), parts of Germany, Switzerland and Italy and a major shifting of European borders. After he lost his power following the battle of Waterloo in June of 1815, he was exiled and the remaining powers under the leadership of Metternich (see above) saw to the dissolution of his legacy, to varying degrees of success.

National Aeronautics and Space Administration (NASA).

Established in 1958 by the United States government, NASA is the preeminent space exploration agency in the world; its most noted previous accomplishment being the placement and safe return of man on the moon. It has served as a powerful outer space research institute and has no official military functions.

National Interest **magazine.**

Founded in 1985, it is an American magazine that publishes news on international affairs and books. Sometimes criticized for its pro-American stances, it is a live example of realist analysis of international affairs: see http://nationalinterest.org/

National Security Agency (NSA).

Formed in 1954, the NSA is responsible for gathering surveillance and intelligence for the United States government and in turn for preventing penetration of US government networks. After one of its former agents, Edward Snowden, published internal documents which revealed some of its espionage activities on US citizens and foreign countries' internet activities in 2013, the organisation was mired in international scandal and Snowden was charged with treason; he was subsequently offered immunity by Russia.

Neocolonialism.

This is the name given to European and American practices as they pertain to a continued subjugation and control of African states; for example, the ousting and killing of Libyan leader Muamar Gaddafi, the presences of French soldiers in Mali and the Central African Republic (CAR), apparently excessive focus on African heads of state by the International Criminal Court (ICC; see above). A highly debated term, it has also been applied to China's policy towards Africa by some scholars.

Neoliberalism.

A name given to a set of economic and political principles which include free trade, privatisation and "rolling back" of state involvement in industry. See also liberalism, structural adjustment programmes, Washington Consensus.

Netanyahu, Benjamin.

Israeli scholar and politician, he has twice served as Prime Minister. The son of a historian and leader of the right-leaning Likud Party of Israel, he has taken a harder line on the Palestinian question (see below) than his predecessors.

Neutral nation.

A state which does not take part in a given war or grant support to either side in an ongoing military confrontation. Switzerland is the country with the longest standing tradition of military neutrality which has been in place since 1815. Other prominent ostensibly neutral nations include Austria (see Austrian neutrality above), the Vatican City-State which has been neutral, though controversially so, since its formation in 1929 and Japan (see Article 9 of the Japanese Constitution above).

New International Economic Order (NIEO).

Adopted in 1974, the New International Economic Order was brought forward by the United Nations Conference on Trade and Development (see below) to institute fairer trade relations between developed and underdeveloped states through the reduction of trade restrictions such as tariffs (see below) and a higher commitment to developmental assistance by the developed nations. The NIEO largely failed as some of its demands, such as the right to nationalise multinational corporations operating in their territories, were deemed impractical. Nevertheless, economic historians acknowledge it as an important signpost in the push for international reform by actors who see themselves as disadvantaged in the north-south dichotomy (see below).

New Partnership for Africa's Development (NEPAD).

An African Union (see above) programme formed in 2001 to enhance economic policy harmony between African states and accelerate development through streamlining funding for infrastructural projects in African states and intra-African trade. Through the African Peer Review Mechanism (see above), NEPAD has also sought to encourage and crystallise good governance, democracy and human rights on the continent.

New Statesman.

British political magazine established in 1913. It is one of the most popular leftist magazines in the world, with regular writers from the left liberal (see above) and Marxist (see above) schools of thought. See www.newstatesman.com

New world order.

A term used by President H.W. Bush in the early 1990s relating to the period which was to follow the dissolution of the Soviet Union and the Gulf Wars in which the west had intervened to defend Kuwait against aggressive neighbour Iraq, under Saddam Hussein. The New World Order, as the President articulated, was to be characterised by international co-reliance and a coordinated shunning and push back against unwarranted aggression by the entire international community.

Nobel Peace Prize.

This is the annual world-renowned prize offered by the parliament elected Nobel Committee to individuals, groups or organisations who have "done the most or the best work for fraternity between nations, for the abolition or reduction of standing armies and for the holding and promotion of peace congresses" and thereby contributed to the realisation of peace. The award is a controversial one, with critics claiming that the choices of recipients are politically-motivated.

Non-Alignment Movement (NAM).

An initiative by India under the leadership of Prime Minister Jawaharlal Nehru, it was a collection of mostly African and Asian states who intended to remain neutral during the Cold War (see above), choosing neither the capitalist US and its allies nor the communist Soviet Union and its allies. Newly independent from colonialism, many of these states were attempting to bolster their recently-gained sovereignty, and at the same time to benefit from both the US and the Soviet Union without alienating the other as most were still developing countries. Other reasons for non-alignment included enmity towards both superpowers, as seen by Iran's self-alienation after 1979 from both sides as the new religious regime under Ayatollah Khomeini deemed them to both be great "Satans" with which alliance was undesirable.

North-South divide.

Refers to the apparent historically and politically rooted economic division between states in the global north, and those in the global south; whereby the global north is characterised by high gross domestic products (GDPs; see above), low levels of debt, high income per capita and high standards of living, the global south – arguably due to exploitation by the global north – is characterised by low GDPs, high national debts, and low income levels and living standards. States said to be in to be in the global north are the US, European states, Israel, South Korea, Japan, Australia and New Zealand.

North Africa.

A geopolitical designation of the states north of the Sahara Desert, mainly composed of Arabized and Muslim populations. This region has had historically more contact with Europe whom it neighbours and easily accessed and communicated with through the Mediterranean Sea. North African states, along with their immediate Arab-majority neighbour states in Asia, form the 'Middle East' with whom they are part of the Arab League (see above).

North American Aerospace Defense Command (NORAD).

NORAD is a jointly operated US-Canada aerospace and air defence organisation that was formed in 1981. Its targets are any airborne military threats to the two states, terrorism as well as drug trafficking organisations.

North Atlantic Treaty Organization (NATO).

Formed after the Second World War, NATO is a security organisation with members in north America and western Europe. With its Supreme Commander always appointed by the US (who also makes the greatest financial and logistical contributions), it has a mutual defence or "injury to one, injury to all" policy. The organisation has partaken in the defending of Albanian minorities in Kosovo, Serbia in 1999, the invasion of Afghanistan following the 9/11 attack in New York and the ousting of Muamar Gaddafi in Libya in 2011. The organisation was once more been brought into relevance by the international crisis brought about by increasing aggression of Russia as seen in the annexing of Crimea under Vladimir Putin.

North Korea.

Its full name being the 'Democratic People's Republic of Korea', it is an East Asian nation formed following the Second World War through Soviet and Chinese assistance against the US backing of allies in the South, it is a "communist" dictatorship under firm control of the Kim family with over 24 million citizens. Eager to forcefully re-unite with South Korea with whom it was once a single country, it has prickly relations with that country and its principal ally, the United States. As of late, especially since the late 2000s, it has engaged in extensive nuclear testing backed with a still anti-America language by the leadership. The UN Security Council (see below) has engineered a multitude of resolutions aimed at imposing sanctions against the country. Nevertheless, it has a powerful ally in the form of the People's Republic of China and has minor but significant trade with the European Union (see above).

Non-Proliferation Treaty (NPT).

Opened for signature in 1968 and effective from 1970, it is an international treaty designed to prevent the further spreading of access to nuclear weapons as well as voluntary discontinuation of possession of nuclear weapons by those states which already have them. Britain, China, France, Russia and the US as states who possessed nuclear weapons before the treaty was formed are recognised nuclear states; India, Israel, Pakistan and Pakistan as well as North Korea who exited the treaty in 2003, are non-members and are generally believed to possess nuclear weapons. See also International Atomic Energy Agency.

Nunn, Nathan.

Canadian economist and professor at Harvard University, his research focus has been the impact of slavery and colonialism on Africa's contemporary economic development. One of his most ground-breaking discoveries has been the lack of trust, and therefore unwillingness to trade, among societies that were the main sources of slaves. Using surveys from the Afrobarometer (see above), he has argued that countries such as Angola, which saw the largest number of people shipped into the Americas to become slaves, are generally mistrustful of the outside world and are therefore less willing to trade.

Oo

Obama, Barack Hussein.

Former US President and the first person of African-American heritage to hold that position; he held it from 2009 to early 2017. His foreign policy initiatives included ending US military presence in Iraq in 2011, but later reinstated it to fight against ISIS in 2014, the elimination of al-Qaeda (see above) leader Osama bin Laden, military intervention in Libya that resulted in the removal and killing of Muamar Gaddafi, the Iran nuclear deal (see above), as well as the Paris Agreement (see below). Critics have spoken against the Yemen drone campaign (see below) which has seen unarmed civilians get implicated, as well as the power vacuum that was ostensibly birthed by the withdrawal of US troops from Iraq in 2011 and gave rise to ISIS. Proponents acclaim his brokering of the Iran nuclear deal, as well as making some steps towards the curbing of US greenhouse emissions. Recipient of the Nobel Peace Prize in 2009.

Oil-for-food Programme (OFFP).

Upon the placement of sanctions aimed at the disarming of the state of Iraq under the rule of Saddam Hussein, there were reports that the sanctions impoverished, and generally negatively affected the civilians of that state more than they did the regime. The United Nations reached an agreement with the Middle Eastern country in 1996 (having initially proposed it in 1995) that it could sell some of its oil strictly in exchange for non-military goods such as food, healthcare resources and educational materials. Profits from the sale of oil were streamed to the French bank BNP Paribas which then directed the money towards Iraq's various obligations such as paying Kuwait for its aggression in the early 1990s, the United Nations peacekeeping forces (see above) and then to the government for purchasing the various basic goods for its citizens. The programme came under criticism over allegations of corruption by Benon Sevan (who headed the programme) and other influential individuals and officials. A report from a commission headed by the former US Federal Reserve Chairman Paul Volcker even questioned the appropriateness of the quality of some of the food brought to be consumed by the Iraqi people.

Oil crisis, 1973.

Refers to the exponential rise in the price of oil per barrel from US$3 to US$12 between October of 1973 and March of 1974 due to an oil embargo against the US by Arab oil-producing states for supporting Israel in the Arab-Israeli Yom Kippur War. It had a negative impact on the US economy and caused the most significant economic drawback since the Great Depression of the 1930s. Politically, it proved that control of oil by those countries which had it could be used for diplomatic gain against the larger superpowers and established OPEC (see below) as an important bargaining institution.

Organization for Economic Co-operation and Development (OECD).

A 35-member international economic organisation, the OECD was formed in 1948 by states who defined themselves as democratic and committed to the pursuit of free trade. The OECD, which is composed of mainly developed states, is a forum for these states to discuss issues of the day and acts as a soft power mechanism to pressure member-states to cooperate on economic, environmental and social issues. The OECD has assisted as a platform for the inception of a number of bilateral tax treaties and action against corruption.

Organization of the Petroleum Exporting Countries (OPEC).

An organisation composed of states which produce and export oil. It was established in 1960 and has 13 member-states. One of its foundational aims is the regulation of oil production for price control reasons so as to increase incomes of its members.

Orientalism.

1978 book by late Palestine-born US activist, literary critic and founder of Postcolonial Studies, Columbia professor, Edward Said. According to the text, an intentionally distorted cultural representation of Asia, particularly the Arab-Muslim Middle East, was formulated by the west with the aim of justifying cruelty, and colonialization by Britain and France in particular and later an imperialist foreign policy by the US towards the region. Criticised by many scholars for various methodological reasons and for making the claim that all western academic investigation on the region is done with the aim of exploitation.

Oslo Accords.

1993 and 1995 negotiated agreement between Israel and the Palestine Liberation Organization (PLO; see below) in which Israel agreed to withdraw its military presence in the Gaza strip and the West Bank and relent to Palestinian self-government in those areas; in turn the PLO formally agreed to acknowledge Israel's right to existence, something which it had until then, along with other pro-Palestine organisations and states in the region, not acknowledged. However, both the Israeli and Palestinian peoples proved unsatisfied with the deal and Israeli Prime Minister, Yitzhak Rabin, was assassinated by an extremist citizen of Israel of Jewish heritage who was opposed to the peace process and protests by Palestinians took a violent turn with the second intifada (see above).

Pp

Palestine.

A highly contested Middle Eastern territory comprised presently of the Gaza strip and the West Bank. It was once a Roman and then an Ottoman province and later a British colony and is now under the de facto control of Israel which has been continually building settlements in the land which was designated for Arab residence in 1948 when the land was turned over to the control of European immigrant Israelites by Britain and the United Nations. Its destiny – be it at the hands of Israel or the Arab Palestinians – is a highly polarising issue in the international community, complicated all the more by accusations of harassment of the Palestinians by the Israeli government and military (Israeli Defence Force – IDF) backed by unflinching financial and moral support of Israel by the US who saw Israel as its main ally in the region in its anti-Soviet Union fight and now its anti-terrorism fight in the region and the sometimes militant activity by those eager for Palestine to be at the hands of Palestinians and become recognised as a country in its own right, as well as the religious significance of the area deemed "holy" in the world's three major Abrahamic faiths, Judaism, Islam and Christianity. So polarizing it is that the issue has seen Israel go to war with various Arab coalitions, most potently in

1967 and 1973 during which times the state has prevailed with external support from its allies.

Palestine Liberation Organization (PLO).

Established in 1964, the Palestine Liberation Organization was founded with the aim of "liberating the Palestinians" from occupation by Israel through armed violence if need be. Nevertheless, it gained observer status in the United Nations (see below) and presently has recognition from about 100 states including Israel as the "sole representative of the Palestinian people." Unlike most pro-Palestinian movements, it acknowledged Israel's right to exist.

Pan-African Parliament.

Established in 2004, it is the legislative arm of the African Union (AU; see above). Its mainly advisory functions are carried out by 10 committees with responsibilities ranging from the environment to trade and immigration-related matters.

Pan-Africanism.

A political and economic school of thought, and general assertion, that argues that African peoples and countries should be united. Adherents differ in the character and extent that this unity should take;

with some taking it to imply a general alliance and cooperation in domestic and international affairs, while others have argued for a literal dissolution of borders and formulation of a single country. Generally used to refer to anything that concerns the entire continent of Africa.

Panama Canal.

A strip of man-made waterway in the central American nation of Panama that connects the Atlantic and Pacific oceans. Originally a French undertaking, US President Theodore Roosevelt facilitated secessionist (see below) elements within the Panama region in the nation of Colombia in 1903 and made the newly independent state of Panama grant the canal to the US which then finished the initial project in 1914. Between then and 1939, Panama was a de facto colony of the US, and until 1999, following a 20-year joint operation of the canal, the canal was under US control. The canal is an important strategic undertaking not only for trade, but also for US national security reasons, as US Navy provisions on the US east and west coasts can be passed back-and-forth through the passage instead of taking the longer route of passing through the southernmost tip of South America in times of need.

Panama Papers.

Refers to the over 11-million documents leaked in April 2016 that detailed use of shell corporations and other means of tax evasion by prominent corporations and individuals through services offered by the Mossack Fonseca law firm based in the nation of Panama. The documents, whose release was facilitate by German journalist Bastian Obermayer, implicated a number of high-ranking political officials including then British Prime Minister David Cameron and Russian President Vladimir Putin (see below) and also usage of the firm to escape international sanctions.

Pariah state.

A state which is regarded as an outsider from the mainstream international community; enjoying little international trade, diplomatic sanctions and similar restrictions on its participation and integration into the international community. This may be due to its aggression, domestic human rights abuses and other acts which divert from prevailing world opinion or preference of states in a power position to impose such isolation on that state. Examples of pariah states have included apartheid South Africa, and present-day North Korea.

Paris Agreement.

An agreement signed by 194 of the world's states in 2015, it is a voluntary commitment to ensure reduction of carbon emissions by the world's industrialised states so that the global average temperature does not increase by 2°C by 2040, it also commits them to donate $100 billion to the underdeveloped countries in order to foster sustainable development path. While good on paper, it has so far proven ineffective due to the fact that it is voluntary, and has received a critical response from the US Congress (see below), many of whose members claim that they believe climate change to not be a real issue or a threat.

Paris attacks, 2015.

A November 13th incident in which ISIS (see above) operatives carried out three suicide bombings and mass shootouts in the French capital city if Paris, killing 130 and injuring 368. The attacks, ostensibly in retaliation of French presence in the war against ISIS in the Middle East, resulted in an escalated French participation in the war against ISIS.

Peacekeeping (PK) forces.

Soldiers contributed by members of the United Nations Security Council (see below), deployed in insistences of violence or protracted civil war or the possibility of these, whose primary purpose is to shelter and defend unarmed civilians. There is controversy and ongoing investigation over alleged malpractices by the PK forces that include allegations of sexual abuse of civilians who are supposed to be under their protection.

Periphery state.

States whose wealth is considerably less than those of core (see above) and semi-periphery states (see below). According to dependency theory, these are the states who are exploited so that their core and semi-periphery counterparts can attain higher standards of living and less dependency. States in this category, by virtue of the international specialisation of labour (see above) which is said to exist by dependency theorists and world systems theorists, tend to be resource-dependent and characterised by political instability. See also North-South divide.

Piketty, Thomas.

French economist and professor at various institutions including the London School of Economics. He entered into public attention after the publication of his bestselling work *Capital in the*

Twenty-First Century in 2013. In the book, the economist showed that the rate of return in wealthy states has consistently been higher than that of economic growth and thereby concluded that the income gap between individuals could only increase in future. Advocate of higher taxes on the wealthy instituted at the global level.

Postcolonial theory.

A form of analysing international relations that bases as its assumption the historical significance, and therefore contemporary relevance, of colonialism as an event and as a legacy. It looks at the continuities of colonialism in today's "post-colonial" world, particularly as they inform the everyday existence of the subaltern (the downtrodden citizens of former colonies) and patterns of the international political economy. A broad field of study with voluminous scholarship, practitioners of this perspective often use non-traditional sources of research such as diaries, novels and travelogues.

Potsdam Conference, 1945.

Taking place on defeated German territory, the conference followed the Yalta conference which had just taken place before. The conference was noted for its agreement on the punishment of Nazi war criminals, and the reversal of Germany's pre-war and war-time territorial gains and German war reparations. It also led to the partition of the German city of Berlin between the powers; in a number of years, the symbolic Berlin Wall would be constructed.

Poverty line.

Refers to the internationally agreed-upon financial figure which the average person in the global population spends per day. The current figure as stipulated by the World Bank (see below) from late 2015 is US$1.9/day meaning that individuals who consume less than this figure per day are said to be living in poverty. Currently, around 10% of the global population live on this amount or less per day.

Powell Doctrine.

Devised by then US military General and later Secretary of State Collin Powell prior to the Gulf War, it is a security policy measure meant to avoid protracted and unpopular war. The doctrine requires it to be ascertained beforehand whether a prospective war is necessary in the first place and whether other means of attaining the objective have failed, whether it will be possible to withdraw and whether the war will receive foreign and domestic support. It differs a great deal from the Bush Doctrine (see above) espoused by President George W. Bush for whom Powell later served as Secretary of State.

Power.

The ability of one entity to cause another to take a course of action it would not otherwise take. In the field of International Relations, it is subdivided into two sorts: hard power and soft power. Hard power refers to the traditional conception of power as based on military and economic capabilities and the use of those who possess these to compel others to act according to a course suitable to their interests. Soft power on the other hand is the use of nontangible means such as diplomacy, "charm" and morality as derived from exemplary behaviour to persuade, and not necessarily coerce, others to act in accordance with a state's preferred course of action. See also hegemony.

Preemptive war.

A national security strategy which involves attacking a state perceived as a threat before it can make a move against the state which ostensibly feels threatened by it. An example includes the invasion of Iraq by the US under President George W. Bush who claimed the invasion was done in order to prevent Iraq, which allegedly had acquired weapons of mass destruction, from attacking the US or arming terrorist organisations such as al-Qaeda (see above), with whom the Middle Eastern state was allegedly allied and sponsoring.

President's Emergency Plan for AIDS Relief (PEPFAR).

Launched by the Bush administration in 2004, a US initiative to curb the AIDS epidemic that hit sub-Saharan Africa from the early 1980s. The programme has spread antiretroviral treatment to close to 8 million HIV-positive people, as well as HIV testing and counselling to more than 56 million people in the continent.

Prisoner's dilemma.

A game theory (see above) scenario in which players assume the roles of two prisoners, who are held in different prison cells and interrogated separately. Offered a shorter sentence if he confesses by himself, but an even shorter sentence if both he and his partner do not confess, each player must decide blindly what to do as he could get a long prison sentence if his partner confesses while he does not. In international politics, this scenario is seen, amongst others, in instances of collective bargaining and military confrontation as each state or institution has only knowledge of what it intends but stands to suffer or benefit by actions taken by their counterpart(s).

Prudential pacifism.

A state's avoidance of war due to the predicted cost that would be incurred from engaging militarily. See also mutually assured destruction (MAD) theory.

Preferential trade agreement (PTA).

An agreement between a group of states to limit trade restrictions such as quotas (see below) and tariffs (see below) between one another but not eliminate them altogether.

Putin, Vladimir.

Russian President between 2000 and 2008 and then again from 2012, having been Prime Minister in the intermediary period. His foreign policy initiatives have included the bolstering of the BRICS (see above) association, and the annexation of Crimea (see above) for which Russia was subjected to sanctions by many states.

Qq

Quota. A limit on the number of goods that may be imported from a particular state, or external states altogether. A protective mechanism aimed at cutting competition for a fragile or new domestic market. See also tariff, customs union, World Trade Organization.

Rr

Realism.

A perspective for analysis of international relations. It has various strands that, while diverging on many important aspects, have common assumptions about the international order. For example, Realists assume that the nation-state is the principal actor in international relations; in turn, Realists assume that the world is in a state of anarchy in which the nation-state is not compelled by any binding higher body. As a consequence, the international arena can be said to be the manifestation of the individual pursuits of their self-interest by all states.

Recession.

An economic figure measured and interpreted differently by various economists and governments that is noted from either reduced economic growth in terms of the state's gross domestic product (see above) or totally negative growth compared to a previous corresponding period. It is seen by some economists as an indicator of general decline of a state's economy, while by others as an incidence of self-correction by the economy after a period of sustained inflation. See also the Great Recession.

Regionalism.

Broad term generally referring to neighbouring states' integration in economic, security, political or other terms. Regionalism can take a minimalist form, such as taken by ASEAN (see above) or a much more integrated form, such as taken by the EU (see above).

Regional trade agreement (RTA). An agreement reached by neighbouring states for preferential trade. Dictated by the conditions and the aims of the parties involved, no two regional trade agreements need resemble one another. Examples of regional trade agreement are the North American Free Trade Agreement (NAFTA) between Canada, the US and Mexico, as well as the European Common Market.

Remittances.

Refers to the flow of financial capital as sent by those living in one country to the country of their origin. An important global economic trend, remittances compose considerable parts of many developing states, and even form greater parts of their GDPs (see above) than any other sector. This is normally used to argue that some gains are made from the so-called brain drain (see above).

Resource curse.

Also called the 'paradox of plenty', it refers to the apparent dilemma posed by relative economic underdevelopment within (especially African) countries that possess vast natural resources. Explanations of this phenomenon vary, with some theories blaming internal mismanagement (see Dutch disease) and other international superpower predation (see dependency theory, Marxism).

Reuters.

British news service established in 1851; one of the oldest in existence. It has a long-standing reputation of reliability for delivering breaking international news. Almost all major news outlets in the world subscribe to *Reuters*.

Right to food.

Refers to the inherent right of people to have access to nutritious food that is obtainable in ways consistent with their right to dignity. It was explicated and put up for commitment by states in the United Nations International Covenant on Economic, Social and Cultural Rights (see below), which has so far gained 164 state parties. While estimates and methods of finding out and measuring differ, more than 1-billion people in the contemporary world are estimated to live in poverty, a figure which is an increase from the 840-million then living in poverty in 1994 when concerted international efforts were put in place to counter it. As an international legal tenet, it remains a controversial issue especially when it comes to how much action the international community can do to counter poverty in a sovereign state that proves either unable or unwilling to prevent poverty on its own.

Rogue state.

A controversial term used to describe a state deemed to be a threat to international peace and security. See also axis of evil.

Roles approach theory.

A form of assessing the foreign policy of a state according to a supposedly self-selected or externally-imposed role that it plays in international politics. Archetypical roles include that of Global Policeman and Mediator.

Rome Statute.

A 1998 treaty which established the International Criminal Court (see above), while the Court began its functionality in 2002. In 2016, three African states – Burundi, the Gambia and South Africa – announced intention to withdraw from the treaty due to the ICC's supposed focus on only Africans for investigation and prosecution.

RT.

Formerly known as *Russia Today*, a global television and online media network established in 2005 and funded by the Russian government, it offers around-the-clock daily news coverage of international affairs as well as documentaries and talk shows which feature the same subject. However, due to its financial ties with the Russian government it has been accused of being a propaganda outlet for the Kremlin, while some welcome its offering of analysis diverged from the somewhat ubiquitous western perspective. See http://rt.com/

Russian annexation of Crimea, 2014.

A 2014 international incident in which the Federation of Russia led by Vladimir Putin (see above) incorporated Crimea, hitherto a part of Ukraine. Initially, Ukrainian Crimea declared itself an independent state and then held a referendum which showed a willingness to join Russia by Crimean citizens; subsequently the incorporation took place upon a treaty between the two entities. As a result of the perceived aggression towards a sovereign state and a prospective European Union member state, the G8 (see above) suspended Russia and the international community posed economic sanctions on Russia.

Ss

San Francisco Peace Treaty.

Signed in 1951 between Japan and the United States and taking effect the following year, in the treaty Japan acknowledged responsibility for the Second World War on the pacific front and acceded to the punishing of those Japanese nationals found guilty of war crimes by the temporary International Military Tribunal for the Far East. The treaty served to relinquish Japan's war-time gains in the pacific; as one of these territories was Taiwan (see below), the problem of Taiwanese independence was retrospectively complicated by the treaty. The treaty also marked the beginning of the friendly US-Japanese relations as the US military has since been virtually in charge of Japan's national security (see Article 9 of the Japanese Constitution).

Scandinavia.

Used to refer to the states of the Scandinavian Peninsula, Denmark, Norway and Sweden collectively. These north European states have a shared history in political, cultural and linguistic terms.

Schengen Area.

Refers to the 1986-established free travel zone that straddles 26 European states in which travellers from the particular states can travel without a passport. Six European Union (see above) member states are not part of the Schengen Area, but four have expressed interest in joining the area; while Ireland and the United Kingdom chose not to be part of the Area. On the other hand, four non-EU states (Iceland, Liechtenstein, Norway and Switzerland) are part of the Area.

Secession.

A scenario in which a territory under the auspices of a sovereign state seeks its own independence. Secessionism in the present times can be observed in the Spanish province of Catalonia (see above), the Indian state of Kashmir (see above), the Canadian province of Quebec, the Belgian state of Wallonia all of whom have large sections of their populations who wish for these territories to be sovereign states in their own right.

Security dilemma.

Refers to the international relations scenario in which states' desire for security paradoxically increase the chances of conflict; when one state increases its military strength, this can be interpreted by other states as a preparation for war, or in any case a move that places their own security in jeopardy, and they in turn increase their own military strength which in its own turn encourages the other state to enhance its military preparedness and so on. Thus readiness for conflict can become a self-fulfilling prophecy because the intentions of each state are effectively unknown by others. It is a classic example of Prisoner's Dilemma (see above).

Semi-periphery states.

States which are neither wealthy and powerful enough to form part of the core (see above) grouping of states, but are nonetheless not so disadvantaged as to be classified as periphery states (see above). According to World systems and dependency theorists, these states are exploited by the core states, and in turn tend to exploit the peripheral states. States in this grouping tend to be middle-income states of some variation, and may be regional powers. Examples of semi-periphery states described by these scholars tend to include Russia, Brazil, Iran, India, South Africa, and Indonesia.

Senkaku Islands.

A small collection of 5 small islands and 3 rocks that measure $7km^2$ that are currently under official Japanese control but are claimed by the People's Republic of China, who refer to them as the Diaoyu

Islands. The islands were placed under official Japanese control upon having been taken from Japanese control following the San Francisco Treaty (see above) and placed under US trusteeship, until 1971 when the US placed the islands under Japanese control under an agreement known as the Okinawa Reversal. According to China's government, the islands are ancient Chinese fishing grounds that were taken from China in the 1890s following the Sino-Japanese War in which Japan emerged victorious. In 2013, the Chinese government launched a new air-defence identification zone which requires all aircraft which are to fly into the zone to comply with Chinese, rather than Japanese, laws and criteria. A complicating factor to the island dispute is the presence of oil and natural gas in the islands, discovered in the 1970s. Another detail which makes the issue particularly pressing is US alliance with Japan, to which it is bound to protect by treaty and recent US reassertions that it will ensure that the islands remain in Japanese control. The islands are placed east of China, northeast of Taiwan and southwest of Japan, and have no permanent human population.

Seoul Peace Prize.

An award presented by the nation of South Korea every two years. The prize is granted to individuals and organisations that are recognised by the committee, composed of 300 Koreans and 800 non-Korean citizens, as having made contributions to "everlasting peace in the world." Previous recipients include German Chancellor Angela Merkel (see above), former Secretary General of the United Nations Kofi Annan (see above), and international non-governmental humanitarian organisation Doctors Without Borders (see above).

Shangri-La Dialogue.

Refers to the Singapore-based yearly summit attended by various heads of state from Europe, East Asia and the pacific. Organised by the International Institute for Strategic Studies, an independent think-tank, the forum has 28 members from the region. The meetings, which take place in the Shangri-La Hotel in Singapore, are usually flanked by important off-record bilateral meetings.

Shi'a-Sunni division.

Refers to the more than thousand-year-old and ongoing division within the Islamic community that led to the formation of two sects, the Shia and the Sunni. Rooted in historical differences that arose in the early foundational decades of the Islamic faith, it has led to strains between various Muslim individuals, organisations, communities and nation-states that are still visible in the contemporary world. A deeply polarising and controversial issue, it has often served as an important factor in the abrasive relations between Iran, which adheres to the Shia branch, and Saudi Arabia, which adheres to the majority Sunni branch (that forms about 90% of the worldwide Muslim population), on many issues including the Syrian civil war (see below), to the effect that Saudi Arabia supports the rebel groups, while Iran supports the regime whose leader is Shi'ite.

Sister city.

A cultural and diplomatic method of "pairing" cities of two different countries and establishing grassroots relations between its local governments and people. Some notable examples of cities with "sisters" in other countries include Tokyo (in Japan) and Seoul (in South Korea), as well as Yalta (in Crimea) and Santa Barbara (in the US).

Slavic. Used to refer to the Slav ethnicity and language group which composes the majorities of some central European, eastern European, south-eastern Europe, north-eastern European, north Asian and central Asian states such as Poland, the Czech Republic, Slovakia, Russia, Belarus, Ukraine,

Serbia, Croatia, Bosnia, Macedonia, Slovenia, Montenegro and Bulgaria. The Slavic peoples have a long and implicative history in European and international relations. For example, the First World War was sparked in large part by the question of Slav nations under Austrian domination in the early 20th century, and the 2014 annexation of Crimea by Russia (see above) has been mired in issues of language and ethnicity within the Slav grouping itself. Slavs are the largest ethnicity in contemporary Europe; with Slav populations making up the majorities in more than half of present-day European states.

Smuts, Jan.

South African military general and statesman, he is the only person in the world to have signed both the preambles of the League of Nations (1920; see above) and the United Nations (1945; see below); having been voted out of and back into power as the South African Prime Minister in the two decades of the interwar period (1918-1938). He presided over a system of racial segregation and domination by whites over blacks in South Africa which preceded Apartheid. He was allegedly designated to be the British Prime Minister in the event that Winston Churchill died during the course of the Second World War.

Socialist Internationale.

Formally established in 1951, the Socialist Internationale is an international coalition of socialist and social democratic parties from different states in the world. Prominent members include the British Labour Party, the Mexican Institutional Revolutionary Party, and the South African African National Congress (ANC).

Soft power.

Refers to the use of attraction and persuasion, as opposed to coercive means such as war or sanctions, by one state to lead another state into following a course of action that is in its best interest. Introduced and articulated by Robert Nye in 1990, it has become a mainstay of international relations analysis and has even been incorporated into foreign policy (see above) formulation. Various publications and institutions maintain and publish regular soft power indexes which are designed to indicate the soft power rankings of states and/or cities.

South African Institute of International Affairs (SAIIA).

Based in the University of the Witwatersrand, Johannesburg, SAIIA is the most prominent International Relations think-tank in Southern

Africa with research focuses including the politics of international trade, global governance, aid and development.

Southern African Development Community (SADC).

A grouping of countries in the southern African region, it is composed of states from South Africa through to the Democratic Republic of Congo. These states seek to use their regional proximity to enhance trade, foreign policy and disaster relief. Founded during the height of apartheid in South Africa to try and build a cohesiveness and self-sufficiency which would allow the "frontline" African states to escape the trade dependency they came to have with regards to South Africa, and to be able to stop trade with the regime which was oppressive towards non-white ethnicities.

Southern African Customs Union (SACU).

The oldest customs union (see below) in the world still in existence today (it was established in 1910). It is composed of the Republic of South Africa, Botswana, and the kingdoms of Lesotho and Swaziland.

South Asia.

A geographical and geopolitical region generally understood to be composed of Afghanistan, Pakistan, India, Bangladesh, Bhutan, Sri Lanka, the Maldives and Nepal. As a region, it has the highest population levels and the states are part of the South Asian Association for Regional Cooperation, initiated in 1985 to facilitate policy coherence and partnering in some objectives by the original 7 states, which later admitted Afghanistan in 2006.

South Asian monsoon.

The climatic phenomenon of reversals in the direction of the wind from the Arabian sea to in the Indian ocean towards India which blow from the southwest for half of the year and from the northeast for the other half. An important determinant of food output for the year in India, it also affects the nearby economies of Pakistan, Bangladesh as well as Bhutan, Nepal and Sri Lanka.

Southeast Asia.

A geographical and geopolitical region generally understood to be composed of Brunei, Cambodia, East Timor, Indonesia, Laos, Malaysia, Myanmar, the Philippines, Singapore, Thailand and Vietnam. Most southeast Asian states are part of the Association of Southeast Asian Nations (see above).

Sovereign debt.

Refers to the debt owed by the government (as opposed to national debt which is a gross total of debts owed by a state's government, citizens and corporations). It may be owed to domestic lenders or foreign lenders. Controversially, sovereign debt can be sold to third parties by the creditor.

Sovereignty.

The principle that states have a right to self-determination and no external parties have the right to influence their domestic life. An increasingly studied issue, some students of international relations have argued that with the growing interconnectedness of states through trade, travel and technology, the concept is becoming less relevant. See also humanitarian intervention, globalisation.

SS Mendi.

A British warship that was sunk in 1917 during World War I (see below), killing some 647 militia, most of whom were African troops fighting on behalf the British, by whom their home countries were colonised.

Stagflation.

Refers to the simultaneous presence of inflation and high unemployment in a state's economy.

State.

A complex political and economic entity which fulfils the criteria for statehood (see below). Its role as the principal actor in international relations in the wake of globalisation (see above) is a subject of rigorous scholarly investigation as some argue that it is becoming less relevant and others, especially Realists, argue that it is inevitably a principal actor in international affairs.

Statehood.

The criteria which a would-be state must fulfil. These, as promulgated by the Montevideo Convention, include (1) formal recognition by other states with whom relations exist or are possible; (2) a permanent population; (3) a geographical territory and (3) a functioning government. As the first criterion is politicised and the third subject to dispute, a number self-proclaimed states are only partially recognised while some are in conflict with others who claim the same territory; notable examples are Palestine (see above) and Kashmir (see above).

Stiglitz, Joseph.

US Nobel Prize winning economist and former World Bank chief economist turned critic of the institution's methods, he has written a number of books against the bank. These include *Globalization and its Discontents* (2002), *Towards a New Paradigm in Monetary Economics* (2003), and Korean economist Ha-Joon Chang edited the volume *Joseph Stiglitz and the World Bank: The Rebel Within* published in 2001.

Structural adjustment programmes (SAPs).

International Monetary Fund- and World Bank-designed measures to be adopted by states in order for them to acquire loans from the institutions. Began in the 1980s in sub-Saharan Africa, and later introduced in East Asia following the 1997 currency crisis in the region, and in Greece following a debt default by the country in 2009, they have been criticised for making conditions worse when measured in terms of individual income and causing recession. Defenders however suggest that they have a perceptual improvement on immediate economic confidence, which can be a key indicator for prospective foreign direct investment.

Sub-Saharan Africa.

Refers to African states that are located south of the Sahara Desert including island states of Madagascar, Mauritius, the Seychelles, and Sao Tome and Principe. Used in politico-ethnic terms to also denote between the Arabs who reside in the north in large numbers and who tend to have closer ties with the Middle Eastern states than states south of the Sahara (see Arab League) and the Africans who reside in the south in larger numbers. The majority of African states are in the territory south of the Sahara; leading to the region sometimes being described as a sub-continent.

Suez Canal.

A man-made waterway that transverses Egypt, thereby creating a passage between the Mediterranean and Red seas. Its construction began in 1859 under the French Suez Canal Company and it was opened in 1869, later falling under British "protection" in 1888, and is today ran by the Suez Canal Authority. It served to decrease the distance to be travelled by ships between Europe and Asia.

Under international decree, it is open for commercial and military usage to any nation.

Surgical military strike.

An attack supposedly designed to exclusively infiltrate and eliminate legitimate military targets of an opponent, and spare civilians and non-strategic structures and vehicles despite their presence. See also drone strikes in Yemen.

Syrian Civil War.

Beginning with major reforms in the early 2000s by the government of Syria under President Bashar Assad, Syria descended into a civil war began when the regime responded forcefully towards protesting citizens seeking more reforms than were given by the government. The civil war is mainly between forces loyal to the government and break-away soldiers (named the Free Syrian Army) as well as various rebel forces. A complicating factor to the war is US involvement on the side of the rebels through whom it hopes to achieve regime change and Russia on the side of the Assad regime with whom it has strategic ties. In the wake of the power vacuum left in the southwest portion of the country, one of the more fundamentalist rebel forces, ISIS (see above), was able to capture large swathes of land in the country which it adjoined to captured territories in neighbouring Iraq and proclaimed an independent state under strict law based on their interpretation of Muslim scriptures. The civil war has led to a humanitarian crisis and large-scale emigration by over a million Syrian citizens, mainly to Europe where their presence has in turn led to a number of political outcomes within the continent; European Union amnesty to some of the refugees, some of whom turned out to be ISIS-aligned terrorists, has been used to further criticise the European Union (see above) by Eurosceptic (see above) movements and commentators. The Turkish President, Reccep Erdogan allegedly used the crisis to attempt to gain EU Passports (which would give them entry into any EU-member state) for Turkish citizens by threatening to allow millions more Syrians to enter EU territories if the EU did not grant the passports.

Tt

Taiwan.

A contested East Asian island which was established by politicians fleeing civil war from mainland China in 1949 when the Communist Party of China took over, it was originally recognised during the Cold War (see below) by the US and its allies as the only legitimate government of China. Since the 1970s, however, an increasing number of states have stopped recognising Taiwan as a state and have placed their recognition on the mainland People's Republic of China. Designating the province as its province, the People's Republic of China has no diplomatic relations with states that recognise Taiwan as a state as such. But with US military backing, though no formal state recognition for the government of Taiwan, the People's Republic of China has not been able to formalise its claim over the island. The question of Taiwan, like that of Palestine (see above), is one of the major diplomatic issues and territorial disputes of the contemporary era. See also Tibet.

Taliban.

Formally established in 1994 by Muslim clerics, it is a militant fundamentalist movement that claims allegiance to Sunni Islam. It is based in Afghanistan where, from 1996 to 2001 it effectively ruled that country following victory in a (1992-96) civil war that had led to the overthrow of the government, and even gained recognition as the official government of Afghanistan from Pakistan, Saudi Arabia and the United Arab Emirates. In that period, it violently enforced strict religious social codes based on their interpretation of Muslim scriptures. Its total control of Afghanistan was reversed when the US invaded that country in 2001 on its crackdown on terrorist organisations following the September 11 attacks. Since 2006, it has maintained a persistent military insurgency against the US and NATO who have been present in the region since the invasion, and maintains some control over the Afghan countryside. The majority of its financial backbone comes from drug trade of opium (which constitutes 2% of the Afghan GDP), and accusations have been made that Afghan neighbour Pakistan is a source of funding despite official alliance with the US. But according to Pakistan officials, they stopped the funding following the invasion by the US in 2001.

Tariff.

A fee that states sometimes impose on foreign goods that are to be entered into its market. See also free trade agreement, customs union, quota, World Trade Organisation.

Terrorism.

A contested term, it generally refers to acts of violence meant to gain public awareness and sympathy, or fearful acquiescence, with a particular cause or group. Some of its recent incarnations have been the 9/11 attacks (see above) on the US in 2001, the 7/7 attacks in London in 2005, Boko Haram (see above) paramilitary activity in Nigeria.

The Spectator.

British conservative weekly political magazine that advocates for measures that lean towards Euroscepticism (see above), realism (see above) and Atlanticism (see above) in British foreign policy. Established in 1828, it is the oldest English-language magazine in the world. Previous editors include Boris Johnson (see above).

Tibet.

Officially under the administration of the People's Republic of China since 1959, the territory is the subject of contestation between the government of China and many within Tibet, led by the 14th Dalai Lama who are vying for Tibetan sovereignty as an independent state. A crucial point of debate for both sides is whether Tibet has been self-governing in recent history or not; with those siding with the

Chinese government arguing that the territory was ruled by China from 1271, while those arguing for secessionism (see above) argue that Tibet was an independent state until its invasion by China in 1949. Individuals and organisations that are supporting Tibetan independence have been active and vocal since incorporation into China, with some employing self-burnings as signs of their protest against Chinese rule, while the government of China has reacted decisively against the Tibetan independence movement, labelling many of its leaders and adherents, including the 14th Dalai Lama who presently resides in India and leads a government-in-exile (see above) as terrorists. The Chinese government has also been known to strain relations with states who support the Tibetan independence movement. See also Taiwan.

Tigris River.

A major source of water to three Middle Eastern states, it runs from Turkey through Syria and opens to Iraq. That its source is in northern-lying Turkey, which could close off its flow to its neighbours at any time, is a major diplomatic advantage to Turkey towards its neighbours, symbolised by the Turkish quip that "the Arabs have oil, we have the water let them drink their oil." This has also been used to tactically disadvantage ISIS (see above) who took over large parts of Syria and Iraq.

Total war.

Refers to a large-scale conflict in which states mobilise even their civilian elements for the purposes of combat. Examples of incidences of total war are World War I (see below) and World War II (see below) in which civilian targets were usually not spared.

Trade deficit.

An economic scenario whereby a state imports more goods and services than it exports in a given year.

Trade surplus.

An economic scenario whereby a state exports more goods and services than it imports in a given year.

Transnational organised crime.

Refers to crime organised and carried out by individuals or groups in various sovereign states. Examples of transnational organised crime include human trafficking, drug trafficking, money laundering and cybercrime. A connection between terrorism and transnational organised crime has been investigated and can be said to exist; for example, terrorists get their military armaments from transnational organised criminals, and the Taliban has been found to get its financial apparatus through drug trade in opium.

Transnational social movement (TSM).

An organisation with members across borders and who share a common cause and desire and work towards a certain end. Transnational social movements differ a great deal in terms of their organisation and their desired ends, but many traits tie them together; for example, they tend to have a perception of an injustice which needs immediate addressing whether it is economic, political or climatic and they usually have an anti-establishment perspective that normally culminates in protests and support for various forms of dissention against the status quo. Examples of some of the most noted transnational social movements include Amnesty International (see above), Greenpeace (see above), and the World Social Forum (see below).

Transparency International.

German-based international non-governmental organisation that specialises in the detection, publicising and combatting of corruption worldwide. Maintains an annually updated list and ranking of corruption by states. See www.transparency.org

Treaty.

A agreement made between two or more states whose terms differ according to the context and the contents of the treaty in question. Treaties can range in their aims; with some detailing a conclusion to a war (e.g., the Treaty of Westphalia; see below), and others specifying terms of investment (see bilateral investment treaty). Nominally, only the head of state or their official representatives may sign a treaty on behalf of their country. There is ongoing debate on whether a change in government relinquishes the state's entry into a given treaty.

Turner, Ted.

US businessman and philanthropist, he founded TBS and CNN. In 1997 he made a donation of $1-billion to the United Nations (see below), which helped set up the United Nations Foundation.

Uu

United Nations (UN).

Established in June of 1945 towards the end of the Second World War, it is the largest and perhaps the most important intergovernmental organisation in present international relations. Formed to prevent conflict, it has assumed more responsibilities along developmental and judiciary lines. The foundational and governmental document of the United Nations is the United Nations Charter (see below). The United Nations has 6 principal organs: the United Nations General Assembly (see below) composed of representatives of all member states, the United Nations Economic and Social Council (ECOSOC; see below), the United Nations Security Council (UNSC; see below), and the International Court of Justice (ICJ; see above), the Secretariat (see below), and the now defunct United Nations Trusteeship Council (see below) which was folded in 1994 after Palau gained independence. The United Nations has been the subject of controversy; present-day critics argue that because of the Security Council's politicisation and history, it is unfair towards underdeveloped states, as well as to states such as Japan and Germany which have assumed importance since the 1940s but are not granted positions reflective of their status; critics also point out that the Secretariat has never been ran by a woman.

Others claim that the veto power held by each of the Security Council members renders the organisation ineffective except for those areas where all states can agree; thus, it is said, this makes the organisation subordinate to political interests of these states. These and many other points have been suggested as areas that need attention and reform in the organisation. Still others commend the organisation for its work against colonisation, human rights abuses, poverty, disease, and conflict and thus deem it much more successful than the League of Nations (see above) which was its predecessor. The United Nations received the Nobel Peace Prize (see above) in 2001 along with its then General Secretary Kofi Annan (see above). Headquarters based in New York City with operating offices in Nairobi, Geneva, and Vienna.

United Nations Charter.

The founding and governing document of the United Nations, it was first signed on June 26 1945 by 50 states and has today been signed and ratified by 193 member-states. It entered into force in October of that year. Its various articles detail the workings of the organisation as well as the member-states' obligations, with it being stipulated in article 103 that obligations to the UN come before obligations to any other treaties (see above) to which the member-state is party.

United Nations Children's Fund (UNICEF).

Established in 1946, the United Nations Children's Fund is the preeminent organ of the United Nations that deals with improving the plight of children and their caregivers and communities, especially those in the industrially under-developed states. UNICEF provides health-related (vaccines, antiretroviral medicines), feeding, educational and emergency (e.g., shelter) resources to poor communities in which children are negatively affected. It received the Nobel Peace Prize in 1965.

United Nations Conference on Trade and Development (UNCTAD).

Established in 1964, the 194 member state United Nations Conference on Trade and Development is the United Nations' main trade, investment and development office. UNCTAD's activities have revolved around ensuring a flow of investment to developing countries. It gained preferential (zero- or low-tariff; see above) entry for some goods manufactured in developing countries into developed countries through the Generalised System of Preferences.

United Nations Development Group (UNDG).

An umbrella organisation for 32 United Nations (see above) agencies and organisations and 5 additional observers, the United Nations Development Group was formed in 1997 to assist in the assimilation of UN initiatives at individual state levels. It is part of the United Nations Economic and Social Council (ECOSOC; see below).

United Nations Economic and Social Council (UNECOSOC).

The organ of the United Nations (see above) responsible for the formation of the UN's economic and social programmes. It meets once every July for 4 weeks, and is composed of 15 specialised agencies and 54 UN General Assembly-elected three-year term members derived from Africa (18), Asia (13), East Europe (8), Latin America and the Caribbean (13) and Western Europe (13). It maintains various regional commissions.

United Nations Economic and Social Commission for Asia and the Pacific (UNESCAP).

Established in 1947 to facilitate economic cooperation among the states of Asia and the Pacific, it presently has 53 states, including the US, Britain, the Netherlands and France. Like other United

Nations regional commissions, the Economic and Social Commission for Asia and Pacific is headed by a regional Executive Secretary. Its present focuses have been attempting to engineer an environmentally sustainable globalisation and trade, as well as human rights. Headquarters are based in Bangkok, Thailand.

United Nations Economic and Social Commission for Western Asia (UNESCWA).

Established in 1973 to facilitate mutual assistance and economic cooperation in the region, the United Nations Economic and Social Commission for Western Asia has 18 states, including Libya, Mauritania, Morocco, and Tunisia who are also part of the United Nations Economic Commission for Africa (see below). Headquarters are based in Beirut, Lebanon.

United Nations Economic Commission for Africa (UNECA).

Established in 1958, the United Nations Commission for Africa's foundational aim is to facilitate economic cooperation among African states. Has 54 members. Headquarters are based in Addis Ababa, Ethiopia.

United Nations Economic Commission for Europe (UNECE).

Established in 1947, along with the United Nations Commission for Asia and the Pacific, it is the oldest United Nations regional commission still operating. Its foundational aim is to facilitate economic cooperation within the member states. Has 56 members, including the US, Canada, Israel and central Asian states. Headquarters are based in Geneva, Switzerland.

United Nations Economic Commission for Latin America and the Caribbean (UNECLAC).

Established in 1948 to facilitate cooperation among its members, the United Nations Economic Commission for Latin America and the Caribbean currently has 45 members, including Japan, South Korea, the US, Canada, Britain, France, Spain, Portugal, Italy and Germany. Headquarters are based in Santiago, Chile. Raul Prebisch, the Commission's second Executive Secretary, was one of the founding scholars of dependency theory (see above).

United Nations Educational, Scientific and Cultural Organization (UNSECO).

Formed in 1945, the United Nations Education, Scientific and Cultural Organization is a United

Nations agency whose foundational purpose is to enhance international peace and security through active encouragement of cultural and educational reforms throughout the world. A major contributor to rises in the international levels of literacy through its campaigns and programmes, it has also facilitated the preservation of culturally important sites through the World Heritage Site foundation. It is a part of the United Nations Development Group (see above). Headquarters are based in Paris, France.

United Nations General Assembly (UNGA).

One of the six principal organs of the United Nations (see above), and the only one to be composed of all the member-states of the United Nations, it presently has 193 members. Its functions include the tabling and discussion of various issues that affect the world, as well the United Nations itself. It also has deciding authority over the policies to be pursued, the budget to be allocated and the selection of the non-permanent members of the United Nations Security Council (see below) all of which are done through a two-thirds majority; while some decisions are done by a simple majority of 51%. The General Assembly is led by a President in yearly sessions in the General Assembly hall in the United Nations headquarters in New York City.

United Nations International Covenant on Economic, Social and Cultural Rights.

Originally drafted in 1954 and later signed in 1966, this Covenant details party states' obligations to provide fair and compensated labour, health and education to individuals. By 2015, it had 164 party states.

United Nations International Covenant on Civil and Political Rights.

Originally drafted in 1954, adopted by the United Nations (see above) in 1966, this Covenant details party states' obligations to preserve the civil and political rights of individuals; that is, their rights to life, freedoms of religion, speech and assembly, their rights to vote and access fair trial. By 2014, it had 168 party states.

United Nations Secretariat.

One of the six principal organs of the United Nations (see above), it plays a largely a bureaucratic role and is staffed currently by some 40,000 individuals globally. Nevertheless, provisions within the United Nations Charter (see above) such as Article 99 allow the Secretary General of the United Nations to bring to attention of the other United Nations organs and agencies issues that he or she deems important for world peace and human rights.

United Nations Security Council (UNSC).

A powerful 15-member council within the United Nations (see above), it has the US, the UK, China, France and Russia as its permanent members and circulates the other ten seats yearly on the basis of geographical representativeness. (i.e., on any given Security Council, there have to be members from countries in Africa, Latin America, and Oceania to fill the 10 non-permanent seats). The powers of the Council include the ability to intervene militarily in a situation it deems necessary to do so. The Council can make enforceable resolutions through consent; each state has a vote but each state also has the ability to prevent resolutions from passing (*veto* power).

United Nations Trusteeship Council.

Currently composed of the 5 permanent United Nations Security Council (see above) members, its chief duty was the overseeing and preparation for eventual independence of 11 Trustee Territories. With the attaining of independence by the last such territory, the island of Palau (previously under US trusteeship), in 1994 the Trusteeship Council has become inactive, while it maintains a provisional duty to meet when necessary.

United Nations University.

The main scholarly body within the United Nations (see above), it was established in 1973 and is based in Tokyo. As of 2010, it can grant degrees to students.

Universal Declaration of Human Rights.

Created and ratified in 1948, the Universal Declaration of Human Rights is a United Nations General Assembly (see above) declaration on the rights of individuals and the international community's obligation, through the United Nations, to defend them. A drawback to the Declaration is that, although it was a milestone and is held as a standard document through which the rights of the individual are explicated, it is non-binding and may only be enforced by states voluntarily.

Uruguay Round.

Began in 1986 and concluded in 1994, the Uruguay Round of trade negotiations took place between some 123 states. It resulted in the creation of the World Trade Organization (see below), with the General Agreement on Tariffs and Trade forming a cornerstone of the new organisation. It tabled the possible removal of protectionist measures with regards to agriculture and textiles, and introduced novel discussions on intellectual property and trade in services. It was succeeded by the Doha Round of negotiations (see above).

US Congress.

An American law-making body whose 535 members are elected within the country's fifty states and districts, it acts as a balancing force to the executive's (President's) power by being able to *veto* (prevent) the President's proposals in domestic and foreign policy through a two-thirds majority. Hugely important, it is composed of the upper Senate (100 members) and lower House of Representatives (435 members), it can in turn propose domestic and foreign policy initiatives to be carried out or rejected by the President. Some of its most significant acts in the international arena were its acceptance of the declarations of war in the two great wars, the granting of US President Lyndon Johnson powers to do as he saw fit throughout the course of the Vietnam War in the 1960s, its acquiescing in the recognition of 'Red' China over capitalist Taiwan in the 1970s. Highly cautious of giving away US self-determination it has also saw to the rejection and thereby weakening of the League of Nations (see above), the International Criminal Court (see above), and various other international treaties within US jurisdiction.

USA PATRIOT Act of 2001.

A US law whose full title is Uniting and Strengthening America by Providing Appropriate Tools Required to Intercept and Obstruct Terrorism Act, it was introduced in 2001 by President George W. Bush as part of the war on terror (see below). It gave US law-enforcement agencies such as the Federal Bureau of Investigations and the National Security Agency (see above) unprecedented powers to arrest, question, detain as well as the ability to maintain surveillance over any individuals suspected of executing or planning acts of terrorism against the US. It has gained criticism for the perceived abuses of power by the agencies, the perceived enhancement and legitimisation of discrimination against Muslim- and Arab-Americans and visitors into the US, and many of its provisions were deemed unconstitutional by various US courts. Nevertheless, it gained renewal in 2005 from the US Congress (see above) and in 2011 President Barack Obama (see above) extended the act for a further four year period. Critics such as Gore Vidal (see above) decried it as a major breach to civil liberties and argued that it transformed the US into a de facto authoritarian state.

US Department of Homeland Security.

A super department composed of some 24 agencies, it was created in the wake of the 9/11 terrorist attacks (see above) in New York, by the Bush administration. It is charged with detecting, pre-empting and responding to acts of terrorism within and around the US. Thus its jurisdiction is around issues of immigration to the US, customs and border protection, cyber activity as well as health and domestic nuclear armaments. It has been criticised of intrusion on the privacy of US citizens, as well as non-citizens; for example, it is one of its agencies' policy to open letters from outside the US whenever it deems it necessary. Headquarters are based in Washington, D.C.

US National Security Advisor.

The principal advisor to the US President on issues related to national security, the National Security Advisor is the President's main source of information and can be the main guide towards foreign security policy. The National Security Advisor also chairs the National Security Council and the Principal Committee meetings whose other members are the US Secretary of State and the US Secretary of Defense. Prominent previous office holder is Henry Kissinger (see above).

Vv

Venezuelan sanctions. Since 2014, the United States has maintained sanctions on the South American state of Venezuela, with whom it had prickly relations since 1999 after the election of socialist Hugo Chavez (who supported Cuba whom the US had isolated since 1960 after the rise of Fidel Castro), following alleged violent reaction by the Venezuelan government to 2014 popular protests. See also Cuban embargo.

Vidal, Gore. US playwright, novelist, essayist and literary critic, he was one of the most outspoken critics of the US's foreign policy especially its expansionism which began in the late 19th century with the acquisition of Cuba and the Philippines as semi-colonies in 1898 and growing in its zeal following the end of the Second World War. His books include the seven-volume *Narratives of Empire* published between 1967 and 2000, *Decline and Fall of the American Empire* (1992), and *The United States: Essays, 1952-1992* (1993). An original and non-traditional critic in his methods and theories, he made insinuations that the attack on Pearl Harbour in 1941 was encouraged by then US President Franklin D. Roosevelt, and that the Bush administration was aware of the possibility of an attack in New York by al-Qaeda but chose to do nothing because it needed an excuse to invade the Middle East for oil. In his later years, he developed a friendship with the aging former (and last) Soviet Premier, Mikhail Gorbachev.

Ww

W.

A 2008 Oliver Stone film depicting the rise of George W. Bush (portrayed by Josh Brolin) from a bad university student, to failed businessman, to Governor of Texas and finally to become President of the US. Valuable for its biographical detail, it is also a unique look into the workings of the Bush cabinet, and the internal lead-up to the 2003 Iraq invasion. Criticised by some as a caricature of the President, his cabinet and the times, it nonetheless proved to be an accurate enough depiction of some of the incidents leading up to the final decision to invade Iraq; especially Vice-President Dick Cheney's influence towards that decision.

Walloon Movement.

A movement adhered to by a small but vocal minority of members of the French-speaking community of multilingual Belgium whose origins can be traced back to the 1880s, it is characterised by a desire for closer integration with the state of France rather than with Belgium; consequently it is critical of the Benelux Union (see above) shared by Belgium, the Netherlands and Luxembourg. Some sections of the movement have also called for independence for a sovereign Walloon state. Has so far received little popular support, but one of many visible secessionist movements in contemporary Europe. See also Catalan independence movement.

Waltz, Kenneth.

Columbia University professor and international relations theorist, Waltz was regarded as the founder of modern realism. His contributions to the field include nuclear deterrence theory (see mutually assured destruction above), a characterisation of the international system as anarchic, the levels of analysis (see above) according to which the foreign policy of a state may be understood through analysing (1)individual motivations of statesmen, (2) the state itself, and (3) the anarchic international system. He was also critical of the view held by many scholars that globalisation would render the state less relevant.

War crimes.

Refers to war-time crimes which constitute intentional acts of aggression against unarmed civilians such as hostage-taking among non-militant populations, utilisation of child soldiers, rape, infrastructural damage not related to war objectives and torture in times of war, and amongst others. War crimes are prohibited by the Geneva Conventions (see above), and are prosecutable on the international arena through the International Criminal Court (see above).

War on drugs.

Refers to the United States' continued campaign to eliminate drug trade within its borders. Originally conceived of as a domestic campaign, due to the international nature of the trade, it has seen the US increasingly interact with other states in Latin America especially and the war on drugs has had many consequences for the justice systems and national security of those states. US military and logistical involvement in Colombian, Mexican and Honduras's sometimes politically motivated efforts against drug trade and trafficking has been a source of major criticism.

War on terror.

Refers to US military, tactical and political efforts to eliminate terrorism following the 9/11 terrorist attacks (see above) in New York and the Pentagon in 2001. It has seen controversial heightening of activity by US intelligence agencies such as the NSA and the CIA (see above), as well as US military engagement in various parts of the world including the invasion of Afghanistan in 2001, Iraq in 2003, an ongoing drone campaign in Yemen (see above), an ongoing insurgency against ISIS (see above) in Iraq and Syria, al-Shabaab (see above) in Somalia and indefinite detentions of terrorism suspects in Guantanamo Bay (see above) amongst others. The pushback against the Taliban (see above) in Afghanistan in 2001, the execution of al-Qaeda (see above) leader Osama bin Laden in 2011, and the containment of al-Shabaab in the Horn of Africa (see above) have been claimed as victories of the war on terror. Introduced and labelled as such by the George W. Bush administration, the term "war on terror" was owned by the Obama administration which has seen it more appropriate to label it as a fight against organisations perpetrating terrorism rather than the tactic itself. Nevertheless, the US and its allies, both within and outside of NATO (see above), continue the campaign. The war on terrorism remains a dividing one; with some claiming not enough is being done, while others criticise it for going too far in curtailing civil liberties, international law and being conducted wrongly by not addressing the very need for terrorism in the first place.

Washington Consensus.

The neoliberal dispensation (see above) as associated and promulgated by the US, and Washington, D.C.-based Bretton Woods institutions (see above), as part of its foreign policy following the end of the Cold

War (see above).

Western Sahara.

A largely desert area in north Africa measuring around $266,000km^2$, it is officially owned by the state of Morocco but a large strip of it facing the Atlantic ocean is claimed to be an independent state under the name of "the Sahrawi Arab Democratic Republic" by the Polisario Front of which it actually controls about a quarter. The Sahrawi Arab Democratic Republic is partially recognised by up to 40 states within the United Nations (see above), and is a full member of the African Union (see above) while the Arab League states, with the exception of Algeria, have continued to deny the republic formal recognition. A ceasefire was agreed upon by both the Moroccan government and Polisario in 1991 which has been breached several times; most notably in 2005 when increased military activity was reported by the United Nations' then General Secretary Kofi Annan (see above).

Westphalia, Treaty of. Signed in 1648, it formalised after the end of the Thirty Years' War in Europe. The treaty went a long way in establishing the principle which has stood, in theory at least, since then; that no state has right of influence over the internal affairs of another. This is the principle of sovereignty. It also led to the end of the volatile and violent Protestant-Catholic religious uproar in Europe at the time.

White House.

The official residence of the United States President in Washington, D.C. As a phrase it is nominally used by the media and others to refer to the entire US executive branch under the leadership of the President. In policy terms, it is used to explicate the fact that an initiative stemmed from the executive branch as opposed to the US Congress (see above), which forms the distinct legislative branch.

WikiLeaks.

Established in 2006, WikiLeaks is a prominent source of confidential and otherwise unavailable information. A controversial organisation, it has released documents pertaining to government policies, personal information of individuals and other sensitive data. While praised by some for encouraging transparency, it has also been criticised for its selectiveness when it comes to targets; it has spared releasing information pertaining to Russia for example, and in the 2016 US Presidential election released information meant to negatively portray Hillary Clinton, then a candidate for the US presidency.

Wilson, Woodrow.

American President between 1912 and 1920, this former professor and historian at Princeton University led the US during World War I (see below) on the side of the Allies (Great Britain, France, Italy and until 1917 Russia). Seeking a post-war peace which would last, he drew up a comprehensive list of 14 requirements which included independence for the then minor and German- and Austrian-dominated European states of Poland, Serbia, Czechoslovakia, and Yugoslavia along nationalistic lines as well as the formation of the (ill-fated) League of Nations (see above). While his institutions and designs failed in the short-run, his ideas have survived in the long-run and form the internationally-minded US foreign policy, and as a part of the theory known as liberalism, and the body known as the United Nations (see above).

World Bank.

An international lending body established in, in 1945, in the wake of the Bretton Woods Conference (see above) to facilitate loans for the war-ravaged countries of Europe in their reconstruction efforts, it later adopted a posture of neoliberal reform aimed at granting loans to countries only if they agree to make certain changes in their domestic and trade policies. These prescriptions, and in turn the World Bank, have garnered a lot of criticism for their lack of positive effect once implemented and their sometimes negative effects such as further impoverishment and widening of inequality. That the Bank is majority owned by the west, is based in Washington and has so far only been chaired by European and American personnel has been heavily criticised as well.

World Economic Forum (WEF).

An international organisation composed of some of the world's 2,500 leading politicians, academics, businessmen and corporations, it meets once a year in Davos, Switzerland where it discusses issues of the day including poverty, economic development and recently increasingly climate change. Established in 1974, its annual meeting in January is the object of much international media attention.

World Food Programme (WFP).

Established in 1961, the World Food Programme is the United Nations' leading food assistance programme for those unable to produce or purchase their own. Helping to feed an average of 80-million people annually, it is the largest such organisation in the world. A member of the United Nations Development Group (see above). Headquarters are in Rome, Italy.

World Health Organization (WHO). A member of the United Nations Economic and Social Council (see above), the World Health Organization carries out the UN's efforts against disease epidemics, and publishes vital health research and statistics each year in its *World Health Report*. It played an important role in the elimination of smallpox, and is currently one of the leading organisations in the efforts against HIV/AIDS, Ebola, TB and malaria as well as food insecurity in the developing world.

World Heritage Site.

Refers to a natural or man-made location or landmark which has been designated as such by the United Nations Educational, Scientific and Cultural Organization (see above) due to its historic, symbolic and/or aesthetic significance; it is convention, though not enforceable law, that such landmarks be not intentionally destroyed but be conserved as much as possible. A landmark becomes a World Heritage Site upon selection by the 21-member World Heritage Committee elected by the United Nations General Assembly (see above).

World Social Forum.

A transnational social movement established in 2001 with the aim of rebuttal against the World Economic Forum (see above) which it deems an inadequate body for the discussion of problems which plague the world's poorest describing the WEF as "a place where billionaires tell millionaires how poor people live."

World Trade Organization (WTO).

Originally called the General Agreement on Trade and Tariffs, the World Trade Organization was formally established in 1945 and later finalised in 1994 in order to facilitate multilateral international free trade. Like the other two Bretton Woods institutions, the World Bank has been criticised as a politicised organisation used by the industrialised west to deprive and exploit the underdeveloped states. Critics point to the fact that the WTO does not enforce trade liberalisation of goods upon the west and only does so on the poor states of Africa, Asia and Latin America; for example, the organisation makes provisions for the subsidisation of agriculture within the west so that it may not need to import agricultural produce from the rest of the world; so far, only the banana may be exported tariff-free into the US and EU, while they in turn have had a wholesale access to the African chicken market. Established to facilitate free flow of goods bearing testimony to what unmitigated trade and globalisation can do, the WTO has ironically been accused of protectionism.

World systems theory.

A theory within the Marxist school of thought (see above), it argues that the world is arranged such that some states necessarily benefit at the expense of others so that some are bound to be in a state of underdevelopment while others thrive.

World War I (WWI).

The first truly total (see above) and global war, the First World War, or the Great War as it was for some time known, began in 1914 with the assassination of the Austro-Hungarian crown prince Archduke Ferdinand by a bullet from a Serbian nationalist, Gavrilo Princip. The Austro-Hungarian Empire declared war on the Kingdom of Serbia and called on its principal ally the German Empire, whose emperor stated unconditional support for Austria (this is known as the 'blank cheque'), for support while the Russian Empire announced its support for fellow Slavs (see above) in Serbia and began mobilisation of troops. The German

Schlieffen Plan for invading Russia's ally France necessitated that the German troops invade France via Belgium, an action which provoked Britain's entry into the war along with the support of troops and supplies from a vast colonial empire. By 1917, the US which had thus far abstained from the war entered the conflict on the side of Britain, Russia, France, Italy and Japan against Germany, Austro-Hungary, the Ottoman Empire and their allies due to Germany's indiscriminate attack of ships, including those carrying Americans. The war, fought mainly in the trenches and with novel technologies such as tanks, poison gas and flying aircraft was protracted and casualties were increased by the breakout of an influenza epidemic leading to 16-million deaths. The war came to a conclusion with Austro-Hungary's surrender and German defeat in 1918. With the Russian monarchy having been overthrown by revolutionaries in 1917, the war also saw the end of three other once-great empires as Germany was turned into a republic with the king having been forced to abdicate, and the Ottoman Empire and Austria-Hungary having been disintegrated and likewise their monarchs having been made to abdicate their thrones. The ill-fated League of Nations (see above) was established to carry out the task of providing a diplomatic alternative to war for states. The Treaty of Versailles which was the principal treaty for shaping the post-war order further stipulated financial war reparations to be paid by Germany whom the treaty stated as being responsible for the outbreak of the war. German colonies in Africa were divided among Britain and France as 'mandates', and a port in China was handed over to Japan. Likewise former Ottoman territories in the Middle East were divided between Britain and France, and others received independence, but usually with pro-western rulers installed beforehand. Some scholars have suggested that the Great Depression which followed, along with the feeling of humiliation by the Versailles Treaty sowed the seeds of resentment in German society and solidified the rise to the belligerent Nazi party which in 1933 took over Germany and in 6 years began what became World War II (see below).

World War II (WWII).

Beginning when Nazi Germany invaded Poland in 1939, the Second World War lasted from 1939, when Britain (and subsequently its dominions, protectorates and colonies) declared war on Adolf Hitler's Germany, to 1945. By 1940, the Germans had invaded much of Europe and installed a puppet regime in France based in the city of Vichy (hence its historic name as the 'Vichy regime'), and had also prompted the Soviet Union under Joseph Stalin to enter the war by attacking the Soviet Union despite an earlier non-aggression pact between the two heads of state. By the end of 1941, the US entered the war due to Japanese attack on the Pearl Harbour military base in Honolulu, Hawaii. With Germany, Italy, Japan and their allies on one side, and the US, Britain, the Soviet Union, China and their allies on the other, the war was the most atrocious since the First World War (see above) and the deadliest in human history. It came to an end in Axis defeat that began to become apparent with Allied invasion of continental Europe through Normandy, France and a later nuclear bombing of Hiroshima and Nagasaki in Japan. Approximately 50 to 80-million people lost their lives in the war, including 11-million in the Nazi-ran concentration camps alone. In its wake, the global order was shifted and saw the crystallisation of the US and the Soviet Union as the preeminent global superpowers, who in turn engaged in a protracted ideological battle known as the Cold War (see above), and the creation of the generally more effective United Nations (see above) to replace the practically defunct League of Nations (see above), as well as Bretton Woods (see above) organisations such as the International Monetary Fund (see above), and the International Bank for Reconstruction and Development, one of the core institutions of the World Bank (see above). The post-War diminished stature of Britain, France, the Netherlands, Belgium as well as Italy and Japan began the process of decolonisation in Africa, Asia and the Middle East.

Xx

'X Article'.

Written and published anonymously by a US diplomat to the Soviet Union while the two states were still allies, it argued that the Soviets Union was imperialistic and friendship with it not sustainable and therefore made the case for a policy of containment (see above) against the communist state.

Xenophobic attacks in South Africa.

Occurring most notably since 2008, these are ongoing and seemingly spontaneous attacks by South African citizens on foreign nationals, hailing especially from Africa and southeast Asia. It strained relations between South Africa and some African governments, especially Nigeria which briefly recalled its diplomats from South Africa on account of the South African government seemingly doing little to halt the attacks on its expatriate citizens.

Xi Jinping.

President of China since 2012. Some scholarly observers of his presidency assert that he has made further reforms in the Chinese economy and has sought to better position China as a power in the East Asian region through a higher defence budget, and the pursuit of Chinese territorial claims in the region, including the Senkanku Islands and various others in the South China Sea. Maintains a One-China policy with regards to Taiwan (see above).

Yy

Yalta Conference, 1945.

A conference between the "Big Three" victors of the Second World War, Britain, Russia and the US, as represented by their leaders, Winston Churchill, Joseph Stalin and Franklin Roosevelt, respectively. It saw the deciding of the post-war order and geography of eastern Europe – most pressingly, whether Soviet-occupied parts of Poland would become free and re-join the rest of Poland to the west – as well as Soviet Union support for the US in its war against Japan in the Pacific.

Yemen precedent.

When, in 1991, the Middle Eastern nation of Yemen proved unwilling to vote in favour of the resolution which would justify an attack on Iraq, it is said that behind closed doors, the US delegate to the UN told his Yemen counterpart that his vote would be "the most expensive No" his country ever makes in that the US would punish dissent. The term is generally used, therefore, to describe any incident in which there are coercive means used to threaten and coerce smaller states by financial or other tactical means if they do not seem willing to vote with a larger state whose interests are at stake.

Zz

Zero-sum game.

A scenario in which one party must necessarily lose for the other to gain. In international relations, this can be observed in instances whereby the poorer countries bear the brunt of climate change brought about by the industrial activities of economically developed nations.

Zimbabwean economic crisis.

Beginning in the late 1990s and culminating in the late 2000s, this is the ongoing economic situation characterised by rampant unemployment, hyperinflation and national debt in the nation of Zimbabwe. Its causes include bad monetary policy, an attempt at price control and international sanctions posed on the land-locked southern African country for reasons related to a domestic policy of controversial land expropriation and redistribution.

Works consulted and recommendations for further reading

I. The Classics

Clausewitz, Carl von. 1971. *On War*, Princeton University Press.

Grotius, Hugo. [1625]2005. *The Rights of War and Peace* (Edited by Richard Tucker), Liberty Fund.

Hegel, Georg Wilhelm Friedrich. "War and the Spirit of the Nation-State." In *The Ethics of War*, by Gregory M Reichberg, Henrik Syse and Endre Begby (, 542-552. Oxford: Blackwell Publishing, 2006.

Hume, David. 1987. 'Essay on the Balance of Power' in *Essays Moral, Political, Literary* (Edited by Eugene F. Miller), Liberty Fund.

Kant, Immanuel. 1795. 'Perpetual Peace: A Philosophical Sketch.' Available at the Mount Holyoke College website: https://www.mtholyoke.edu/acad/intrel/kant/kant1.html

Malthus, Thomas. [1798]1998. *An Essay on the Principle of Population, as it Affects the Future Improvements of Society and with Remarks on the Speculations of Mr. Godwin, M. Condorcet, and Other Writers*, Electronic Scholarly Publishing Project.

Sun Tzu [circa 500BCE] 2007. *The Art of War.* Colombia University Press.

II. Pioneering Texts

Acemoglu, Daron & Robinson, James. 2012. *Why Nations Fail: The Origins of Power, Prosperity, and Poverty*, Crown Business.

Cox, Robert. 1981. 'Social forces, states, and world orders: Beyond International Relations theory', *Millennium 10(2): 126-55.*

Easterly, William. 2014. *The Tyranny of Experts: Economists, Dictators, and the Forgotten Rights of the Poor*, Basic Books.

Fukuyama, Francis. 1992. *The End of History and the Last Man*, Free Press.

Gibbon, Edward. 1979. *The Decline and Fall of the Roman Empire*, Bison.

Ha-Joon Chang. 2007. *Bad Samaritans: The Myth of*

Free Trade and the Secret History of Capitalism, Bloomsbury Press.

Hobsbawm, Eric J. 1992. *Nations and Nationalism since 1780: Programme, Myth, Reality*, Cambridge University Press.

Huntington, Samuel P. 1996. *The Clash of Civilizations and the Remaking of World Order*, Simon & Schuster.

Morgenthau, Hans. 1948. *Politics Among Nations: The Struggle for Power and Peace*, Alfred A. Knopf.

Morris, Ian. 2010. *Why the West Rules – For Now: The Patterns of History, and What They Reveal About the Future*, Farrar, Straus and Giroux.

Mudimbe, V.Y. 1994. *The Idea of Africa*, Indiana University Press.

Nye, Joseph. 1991. *Bound to Lead: The Changing Nature of American Power*, Basic Books.

Sen, Amartya. 1992. *Inequality Reexamined*, Oxford University Press.

Waltz, Kenneth. 1959. *Man, the State, and War*, Columbia University Press.

III. Introductory Texts

Baylis, J., Smith, S., & Owens, P. 2011. *The Globalization of World Politics*, Oxford University Press.

Cecil, Algernon. 1947. *Metternich: A Study of His Period and Personality*, Eyre and Spottinwoode.

Kissinger, Henry (Editor). 1965. *The Problems of National Strategy: A Book of Readings*, Praeger.

Kurlantzick, Joshua. 2007. *The Charm Offensive: How China's Soft Power is Transforming the World*, Yale University Press.

McMahon, Robert. 2003 . *The Cold War: A Very Short Introduction*, Oxford University Press.

Miller, J., 1966. The Politics of the Third World. London: Oxford University Press.

Munro, J. Forbes. 1976. *Africa and the International Economy, 1800-1960: An Introduction to the Modern Economy of Africa South of the Sahara*, Dent.

Synder, Louis L. 1955. *The World in the Twentieth Century*, D. Van Nostrand.

Strassler, Robert B. 1996. The Landmark

Thucydides: A Comprehensive Guide to the Peloponnesian War. Free Press.

Wilkinson, Paul. 2007. *International Relations: A Very Short Introduction*, Oxford University Press.

IV. Reports

Berg, Elliot. 1981. *Accelerated Development in Sub-Saharan Africa: An Agenda for Action*, International Bank for Reconstruction and Development / The World Bank.

Khilnani, Sunil, Kumar, Rajiv, Mehta, Pratap B., Menon, Prakash, Nilekani, Nandan, Raghavan, Srinathi, Saran, Syham & Varadarajan, Siddharth. 2012. *Non-Alignment 2.0: A Foreign and Strategic Policy for India in the Twenty First Century*, Center for Policy Research. Available at: cprindia.org/research/reports/nonalignment-20-foreign-and-strategic-policy-india-twenty-first-century/

V. General Texts

Aron, Raymond. 1968. *On War*, Norton.

Barker, Rodney. 1990. *Political Legitimacy and the State*, Clarendon Press.

Barnett, Michael & Weiss, Thomas G. 2008.

Humanitarianism in Question: Politics, Power, Ethics, Cornell University Press.

Chabal, P. 1999. *The Politics of Suffering and Smiling*, Cambridge University Press.

De Walle, N. 1999. *African Economies and the Politics of Permanent Crisis, 1979-1999*, Cambridge University Press.

Esdaile, Charles J. 1995. *The Wars of Napoleon*, Longman.

Heinze, Eric. 2009. *Waging Humanitarian War: The Ethics, Law, and Politics of Humanitarian Intervention*, SUNY Press.

Herbst, J. 2000. *States and Power in Africa: Comparative Lessons in Authority and Control*, Princeton University Press.

Huntington, Samuel P. 1986. *American Military Strategy*, University of California Press.

Keohane, Robert & J. L. 2003. Holzgrefe. *Humanitarian Intervention: Ethical, Legal, and Political Dilemmas*, Cambridge University Press.

Khilnani, Sunil. 2003. *The Idea of India*, Penguin.

Markoff, John. 1996. *Waves of Democracy: Social*

Movements and Political Change, Pine Forge Press.

Marks, Frederick W. 1979. *Velvet on Iron: The Diplomacy of Theodore Roosevelt*, Nebraska University Press.

Melvin, Frank Edgar. 1919. *Napoleon's navigation system: A Study of Trade Control During the Continental Blockade*, Pennsylvania University Press.

Midlarsky, Manus I. 1975. *On War: Political Violence in the International System*, Free Press.

Nester, William R. 2010. *Globalization, War and Peace in the Twenty-first Century*, Palgrave.

Nicolson, Harold G. 1946. *The Congress of Vienna: A Study in Allied Unity: 1812-1822*, Constable.

Perkins, John. 2004. *Confessions of an Economic Hitman*, Berrett-Koehler Publishers.

Rathburn, Brian C. 2011. *Trust in International Cooperation: International Security Institutions, Domestic Politics and American Multilateralism*, Cambridge University Press.

Stoessinger, John G. 1990. *Why Nations Go to War*, St Martin's Press.

Vincent, R.J. 1974. *Nonintervention and International*

Order, Princeton University Pres.

Waterlow, C. 1974. *Superpowers and Victims: The Outlook for World Community*, NJ: Prentice-Hall.

Young, C. 2004. The end of the post-colonial state in Africa? Reflections on changing African political dynamics. *African Affairs, 103, 23-49.*

VI. Primary Texts

The African Union. 2014. *Agenda2063: The Africa we Want*. Available at the African Union website: agenda2063.au.int

The People's Republic of China. 2016. 'Five Year Plan, 2016-2020'. Beijing: Government Printer.

The Republic of South Africa. *White Paper on South African Foreign Policy – Building a Better World: The Diplomacy of Ubuntu*. Available at the South African government website: www.gov.za/documents/white-paper-south-african-foreign-policy-building-better-world-diplomacy-ubuntu

Presidents of the United States. 1961. Inaugural Addresses of the Presidents of the United States from George Washington, 1789, to John F. Kennedy, 1961, Compiled by the Legislative Reference Service, Library of Congress, U.S.

Government Office.

United Nations. *The Charter of the United Nations.* Available at the United Nations website: http://un.org/en/documents/charter/

Wilson, Woodrow. 'Fourteen Points'. Available from the Yale University website: avalon.yale.edu/20[th]_century/wilson14.asp

ABOUT THE AUTHOR

Educated at the University of the Witwatersrand, Johannesburg, Bhaso Ndzendze is an award-winning international relations scholar whose other publications include peer-reviewed works on international relations, newspaper articles and books. He is the author of the 2015 book, *Africa: The Continent we Construct*.

www.ingramcontent.com/pod-product-compliance
Lightning Source LLC
Chambersburg PA
CBHW060448280326
41933CB00014B/2696